ROUTLEDGE LIBRARY EDITIONS: LIBRARY AND INFORMATION SCIENCE

Volume 62

ONE HUNDRED YEARS OF SCI-TECH LIBRARIES

ONE HUNDRED YEARS OF SCI-TECH LIBRARIES
A Brief History

Edited by
ELLIS MOUNT

LONDON AND NEW YORK

First published in 1988 by The Haworth Press, Inc.

This edition first published in 2020
by Routledge
2 Park Square, Milton Park, Abingdon, Oxon OX14 4RN

and by Routledge
52 Vanderbilt Avenue, New York, NY 10017

Routledge is an imprint of the Taylor & Francis Group, an informa business

© 1988 The Haworth Press, Inc.

All rights reserved. No part of this book may be reprinted or reproduced or utilised in any form or by any electronic, mechanical, or other means, now known or hereafter invented, including photocopying and recording, or in any information storage or retrieval system, without permission in writing from the publishers.

Trademark notice: Product or corporate names may be trademarks or registered trademarks, and are used only for identification and explanation without intent to infringe.

British Library Cataloguing in Publication Data
A catalogue record for this book is available from the British Library

ISBN: 978-0-367-34616-4 (Set)
ISBN: 978-0-429-34352-0 (Set) (ebk)
ISBN: 978-0-367-36334-5 (Volume 62) (hbk)
ISBN: 978-0-367-36336-9 (Volume 62) (pbk)
ISBN: 978-0-429-34536-4 (Volume 62) (ebk)

Publisher's Note
The publisher has gone to great lengths to ensure the quality of this reprint but points out that some imperfections in the original copies may be apparent.

Disclaimer
The publisher has made every effort to trace copyright holders and would welcome correspondence from those they have been unable to trace.

One Hundred Years of Sci-Tech Libraries: A Brief History

Ellis Mount
Editor

The Haworth Press
New York • London

One Hundred Years of Sci-Tech Libraries: A Brief History, has also been published as *Science & Technology Libraries,* Volume 8, Number 1, Fall 1987.

©1988 by The Haworth Press, Inc. All rights reserved. No part of this book may be reproduced or utilized in any form or by any means, electronic or mechanical, including photocopying, microfilm and recording, or by any information storage and retrieval system, without permission in wrting from the publisher. Printed in the United States of America.

The Haworth Press, Inc., 12 West 32 Street, New York, NY 10001
EUROSPAN/Haworth, 3 Henrietta Street, London WC2E 8LU England

LIBRARY OF CONGRESS
Library of Congress Cataloging-in-Publication Data

One hundred years of sci-tech libraries : a brief history / Ellis Mount, editor.
    p. cm.
    "Also . . . published as Science & technology libraries, volume 8, number 1, fall 1987" — T.p. verso.
    Bibliography: p.
    ISBN 0-86656-745-3
    1. Scientific libraries — United States — History. 2. Technical libraries — United States — History. 3. Library science — United States — Hisotry. I. Mount, Ellis. II. Title: One hundred years of science-technology libraries. III. Title: 100 years of sci-tech libraries.
    Z675.T3053   1988
    026'.50'973-dc19   87-34567
                                                                                                                                CIP

One Hundred Years of Sci-Tech Libraries: A Brief History

CONTENTS

Introduction	1
Academic Scientific and Technical Libraries: Some 19th and 20th Century Tales	3
Karla J. Pearce	
Introduction	3
Collections	4
Departmental Libraries: Convenient but Costly	7
The Future	11
Science and Technology Departments in Public Libraries: A Review of the Past Century	17
Jean Z. Piety	
Evelyn M. Ward	
The Beginnings	17
The Turn of the Century	20
After World War II	28
Scientific and Technical Libraries in the Federal Government: One Hundred Years of Service	35
Sarah Thomas Kadec	
Carol B. Watts	
Introduction	35
Studies	36
Early Beginnings	38
Increased Development	39
Departmental Libraries	40

Independent Agencies	42
The National Libraries	43
Trends in Federal Scientific and Technical Libraries and Information Centers	43

Corporate Science and Technology Libraries: One Hundred Years of Progress — 51
Edythe Moore

Early Development: Pre-World War I	52
World War I – 1940	54
Post-World War II	56
1988 and Beyond	58

Information-Retrieval: A 35-Year Personal Perspective — 61
Everett H. Brenner

I. Accountability and Responsibility	62
II. An Approach to the Computer World	63
III. A National Plan for Abstracting and Indexing Services?	66
IV. Information Environments	69
V. Brenner's Laws of Information Science	73

Education for Sci-Tech Librarianship: Retrospect and Prospect — 75
Linda C. Smith

Retrospect	76
Current Trends	83
Prospect	83

SPECIAL PAPER

Statistical Data for Stand-Alone Science/Engineering Libraries in the United States and Canada 1984/1985 — 89
Emerson Hilker

Background	89
Membership	90
Tables	91

SCI-TECH COLLECTIONS 129
Tony Stankus, Editor

CAD/CAM (Computer-Aided Design/Computer-Aided Manufacturing): A History of the Technology and Guide to the Literature Part II 131
Colette O'Connell

Appendix 1: Acronym Glossary	132
Appendix 2: Classified CAD/CAM Bibliography	134
Appendix 3: Associations and Societies	160
Research Centers	162
Online Venders	164

NEW REFERENCE WORKS IN SCIENCE AND TECHNOLOGY 169
Robert G. Krupp, Editor

SCI-TECH IN REVIEW 187
Karla Pearce, Editor
Giuliana A. Lavendel, Associate Editor

Introduction

In 1887 a class of seventeen women and three men assembled in an unused storeroom over the Chapel at Columbia University, ready to begin a course of instruction in librarianship.[1] This humble beginning of what was then called the School of Library Economy, created by Melvil Dewey, marked the inauguration of the first library school in the United States. It was Dewey's vision of the need for formal education for librarians which brought about the creation of the school. Now, with dozens of library schools in existence, having thousands of graduates each year, it is easy to forget the difficult time Dewey had in opening and maintaining this school. It seems only appropriate at the one hundredth anniversary of the founding of the first library school to dedicate this volume to the memory of Melvil Dewey. His pioneer efforts deserve more than casual recognition. Our profession can profit from emulating the foresight and concerted effort exemplified by Dewey.

The theme of this book is "One Hundred Years of Sci-Tech Librarianship." It aims at providing a survey of the development of sci-tech libraries as well as some thoughts about their future. As can be seen from the table of contents, this volume covers several types of sci-tech libraries, information retrieval, and library education. Collectively these papers present a fairly broad picture of the role of sci-tech libraries during the past hundred years of librarianship.

The history and growth of academic sci-tech libraries are discussed in a paper by Karla J. Pearce, while public library departments devoted to science and technology are covered in a paper by Jean Z. Piety and Evelyn M. Ward.

Sci-tech libraries serving the federal government are discussed in the paper by Sarah Thomas Kadec and Carol B. Watts, while Edythe Moore describes the development of corporate sci-tech libraries and information centers.

A perspective on the development of computerized information retrieval services over the past 35 years is found in the paper by Everett H. Brenner. The history of the education for sci-tech librarianship is the subject of the paper by Linda C. Smith.

One of our special papers for this issue consists of an extensive statistical survey of the operational data from twenty-three academic science and engineering libraries belonging to the Association for Research Libraries (ARL). It was compiled by Emerson Hilker. The other special paper is part two of a survey of the literature on computer-aided manufacturing and design, prepared by Colette O'Connell.

Our regular features complete the issue.

Ellis Mount
Editor

REFERENCE

1. Trautman, Ray. *A history of the School of Library Service, Columbia University*. New York: Columbia University Press; 1954.

Academic Scientific and Technical Libraries: Some 19th and 20th Century Tales

Karla J. Pearce

SUMMARY. Anecdotes about late 19th and early 20th century collectors and libraries illustrate the beginnings of some of our more notable academic scientific and technical libraries. These are followed by a discussion of some of the opportunities that new technologies are offering for the future.

INTRODUCTION

In 1886, in an address to the Association of Collegiate Alumnae, Melvil Dewey said:

> The colleges are waking to the fact that the work of every professor and every department is necessarily based on the library; text books constantly yield their exalted places to wiser and broader methods; professor after professor sends his classes, or goes with them, to the library and teaches them to investigate for themselves, and to use books, getting beyond the method of the primary school with its parrot-like recitations from a single text. With the reference librarians to counsel and guide readers; with the greatly improved catalogs and indexes, cross-references, notes and printed guides, it is quite possible to make a great university of a great library without professors. Valuable as they are in giving person inspiration,

---

Karla J. Pearce is Assistant Director, Science and Engineering Division, Columbia University Libraries. She has an A.B. from Radcliffe College and the M.L.S. degree from the University of Pittsburgh.

© 1988 by The Haworth Press, Inc. All rights reserved.

they can do little in making a university without the library. Just as truly as we found in popular education that the real school for the mass of people, and for all their lives except early childhood, was the library, so in the higher education the real university is a great library thoroughly organized and liberally administered.[1]

Dewey was a man of vision and great ambitions for libraries. Today, just over a century later, most librarians would probably not recognize his dream as their reality, even those who work in the areas devoted to the areas of liberal arts that Dewey had in mind. For librarians of scientific and technical libraries, the vision may be even more blurred.

The stories of scientific and technical libraries in the late 19th and early 20th centuries, the time of Melvil Dewey's career, are tales of pioneers. Although we are separated from them by a time that has seen enormous change and growth, their problems are still familiar to us today.

Acquiring and maintaining collections; meeting the needs of our primary and constant users without cheating the casual researcher; meeting the research needs of the institution served by the library in an economic and efficient manner: these were some of the challenges noted by late 19th century scientific and technical librarians and their historians.

What follows is more anecdotal than scientific, and, like all history, is taken from accounts that may be biased; but it gives a "snapshot" of academic libraries serving the needs of science and technology before the World Wars. It is followed, in the spirit of Melvil Dewey, with some modern-day plans and ideas for the century coming up.

COLLECTIONS

Academic science libraries were, and still are, defined by their collections. Universities rarely went out to purchase large scientific collections. Those funds were usually reserved for the great works of history and the humanities. Hundreds of academic science collections began as small or large, lovingly collected private science collections. With great respect for the forgotten stewards of these early libraries, it is the collections and collectors who are usually memorialized. Asa Gray, Father Julius Nieuwland, and Joseph Branner were just three of a long and distinguished list of dedicated scholars/researchers whose collections formed the beginnings of great university science libraries.

Asa Gray

Asa Gray's story might be considered to be pure 19th century Americana. He was born in 1810 in Oneida County, New York, on what was then the American frontier, eldest son of a farmer-tanner. He studied science and received his medical degree from a local academy, but his interest in botany and mineralogy grew and after a short time, he began to make his living teaching courses in those areas. Gray used the money he had earned teaching to finance excursions to collect plant specimens in New York and New Jersey. His work caught the interest of Dr. John Torrey, who worked with him and encouraged his research until he became Curator of the New York Lyceum of Natural History in 1835. He was appointed to teach botany at the University of Michigan, but some state financial problems postponed that appointment, so he accepted instead an appointment to be Fisher Professor of Natural History at Harvard, in 1842. There he began to amass in earnest his library and herbarium.[2,3]

Asa Gray is known for his pioneer work as a natural systematist, for his training of teachers of botany, for his early belief in Darwin's theory of evolution and for assembling a great botanical collection. On an annual salary of $1,000, meager even in those days, Gray managed:

> with absolutely no property of his own, to bring together a large library and to create an admirable herbarium. The small house in the Garden in which he had lived at last became so crammed with books and plants that it might almost be said that guests had to sleep on plants, and that the china closet had become a library.[2]

Concerned that a fire might destroy it, in 1865 Gray presented his collection to Harvard College, at which time it numbered a minimum of 200,000 specimens and about 2,200 books, not including pamphlets. For the first time students and researchers had access to materials of early explorers and botanists, synthesized and gathered into a "compact and comprehensive whole."

Julius A. Nieuwland, CSC

Julius Arthur Nieuwland was born in Hansbecke, Belgium, in 1878, and emigrated with this family to South Bend, Indiana, 2 years later. As a child he showed a great interest in and aptitude for science, particularly botany, and began collecting specimens at an early age. After graduating from the University of Notre Dame in 1899, he went to Catholic University in Washington D.C. where, in 1904, he earned a PhD with chemistry as his major and botany as his minor. His dissertation, "The Reactions of Acetylene," described the chemical research that he continued throughout his career although he continued doing substantial research in both chemistry and botany.

With an interest in the taxonomy of ferns and flowering plants, he collected specimens throughout Indiana and Michigan. He built up a fine historical collection, supporting it with funds he earned from the manufacture and sales of microscopic preparations of histological objects for botanical research. His dedication to collecting was well known, and he apparently was not shy about involving others in that quest. According to one story, on an automobile trip a friend tried to drive very fast so that Father Nieuwland would not be able to spot any unusual flora or fauna, but he couldn't go fast enough. Despite the speed, Father Nieuwland had spotted a new plant along the road, and he insisted his friend drive back five miles to get it.

But it was for his contributions to chemistry that Father Nieuwland is probably best known. Chemists at DuPont had been trying unsuccessfully throughout the period around the First World War to synthesize a material that would substitute for natural rubber. In 1925, at an American Chemical Society meeting some people from Dupont heard Father Nieuwland describe his research on the catalytic polymerization of acetylene, and they realized its commercial possibilities. DuPont contracted with him for this process and for his services as a consultant. Building on his research, they were able to synthesize Neoprene, which became the first practical rubber-like material that would do everything that rubber would do. And with the money he received from DuPont, Father Nieuwland purchased the serials and monographs which were the beginnings of the excellent chemistry collection at the University of Notre Dame.[5,6,7,8]

John Caspar Branner

Stanford University, founded in 1891, also suffered in those early days from inattention to library acquisitions for the sciences. John C. Branner, Professor of Earth Science and Stanford's second president, maintained for his and his students' use, his own personal library. The university spent almost nothing on geology and very little on mining, metallurgy and mineralogy. In 1914 he sold this collection to Stanford, for what the books had cost him, and it became the foundation for the Branner Library.

Among the reasons for the library's budgetary difficulties were cash flow problems brought about by probate of Leland Stanford's estate. Faculty suffered salary cuts and all library acquisitions fell. Concerned with the problems this was causing, Stanford's widow, Jane L. Stanford, established in 1906, what became known as the Jewel Fund. She directed that all of her jewels be sold after her death and the money used to support the university. The money from the sale was to go first to build the Stanford Church. After that, it became an endowed book fund for the libraries.[9]

DEPARTMENTAL LIBRARIES: CONVENIENT BUT COSTLY

For reasons that are all too clear to those of us who have worked in modern departmental libraries, this was, and still is, our users' organizational pattern of choice. Since their libraries had often begun attached to scientific laboratories, engineers and scientists grew to depend on having needed resources close at hand.

But to those not involved in scientific research, the concept was harder to justify. In a convincing little pamphlet published by the Massachusetts Institute of Technology for the Columbian Exposition of 1893, the author extols MIT's mission of producing graduates who are well-educated men first, engineers second. In a section on the libraries, the departmental organization is defended. It explains that "books are regarded as apparatus for immediate use; and the collections are, therefore, placed in direct connection with the several departments."[10]

Another account by the MIT Librarian, 23 years later, shows a less idealized perception:

> It was the hope of President MacLaurin and of the Librarian that in the new Central Library any officer or student would find there, with a minimum of effort, any book or set of journals belonging to the Institute, whatever the subject might be. The departmental libraries were to be limited to current periodicals and books needed frequently for quick immediate reference. That hope was not to be realized. In the first place lack of a sufficient building fund had forced the Electrical Engineering Department into space intended for the Library, and the Library had been pushed into the dome. Then tradition was too strong. Biology and Electrical Engineering remained in the Central Library but other departments not so near wanted separate libraries. So departmental libraries grew and the Central Library was becoming merely the business office of the system and a depository for old sets of journals and other little used books.[11]

In an interesting side note on the collections of those days, the Columbian Exposition pamphlet brags that in 1893 MIT's periodical subscriptions, excluding annuals, number 362, making it "one of the largest collections of scientific journals, magazines and reviews to be found anywhere."[12]

This choice of branch libraries to support individual academic departments appears to have been as controversial in those days as it is today. In an account from the "Report of Departmental Libraries," University of California, 1916, Harold Lempp noted that although there had been some improvement in the departmental libraries, they were still:

> unsatisfactory because of of poor housing, inadequate space, absence of reference books, lack of staff and irregular hours. Annual inspections required by the California State Board of Regents revealed considerable disorganization and poor management.[13]

Instead of being alarmed by this, the Chemistry Faculty subsequently requested transfer of "a large number of periodical files and journals to its collections from the General Library." The Library committee recommended against this, recognizing that this would not only detract from the General Library's collection in Chemistry but possibly would encourage other departments to make similar requests. Therefore, the Academic Senate established:

> the general policy of maintaining a comprehensive central collection of books as against the distribution of these in departmental libraries, and of limiting the withdrawal of books and periodicals for deposit in departmental libraries to those which are exclusively used by the departments concerned and which are replaceable in case of loss.[14]

Plus ça change . . .

Most of the great collections of science and technology that now serve academic users, e.g., the John Crerar and Linda Hall Libraries, were actually chartered as public libraries. If these anecdotes are at all representative, the majority of nineteenth century libraries dedicated to supporting academic programs in science and technical studies did not benefit from great endowments. They faced the same pressures we do today to justify costs, find more space, and prove their efficiency. Sounding very much like a director of an academic library, in a 1926 speech to the American Library Association, Dewey noted:

At the recent meeting of the British Association, it was said "the greatest concern of scientists is about cemeteries and libraries." Cremation solved the problem of growing cemeteries, but the mind is appalled to see what will be later when there are now 23,000 scientific periodicals published every year.[15]

People who administered the library funds (usually successful businessmen) found it hard to understand why more than one of these very expensive serial subscriptions was needed. In 1888, President Walker of MIT defended to the board of trustees the extra costs incurred in duplicating collections in departmental libraries:

> I do not think it would be an exaggeration to say that the use of books by our students is fourfold what it would be if the students were required to go to a large general library and take out the desired volumes with the formalities usual in such cases. With us, books are tools for handy use; just as much so as the apparatus of the chemical or physical laboratories.[16]

Other businessmen probably agreed with the doubters. Andrew Carnegie, who donated funds to build 2,811 libraries, did not see the need to provide a library for the students at the Carnegie Technical Schools that he founded in Pittsburgh. He and his advisors felt that the 8-minute walk to the Carnegie Institute of Pittsburgh, with its strong technical division, did not justify giving Tech students their own library. In 1937, with heartrending detail, President Tarbell describes the former YMCA canteen, known as the "Hut," that had become the Carnegie Tech library:

> It is a squat, one story affair, with uncertain foundations, wooden walls. . . . By frequent application of paint it endeavors bravely, though unsuccessfully, to hold its own in the more pretentious architectural company it keeps.
> Obviously built for the duration of the war, one of these slight shelters became absent with leave when the soldiers left, but the other was acquired by the college, moved to its present site, opened on January 6, 1920, and has since become one of the smallest and humblest libraries in the land.

Some day, and let it not be too far distant, a suitable library will doubtless come, and then the war relic, this little green anachronism in our midst, will pass into oblivion, unregretted and unsung.[13]

It was demolished in 1945.

THE FUTURE

It's pleasant to memorialize our pioneers and sympathize with their problems. But have we any solutions? Are we approaching Melvil Dewey's vision, here slightly edited, that the "real [scientific and technical] university is a great [scientific and technical] library, thoroughly organized and liberally administered"? Is this a "possible dream?"

A statement on the library's expanding role in the provision of information was delivered by Jay Lucker, Director of Libraries, Massachusetts Institute of Technology, in his keynote address to the International Association of Technological University Libraries in June 1985.[18]

He noted the revolutionary changes that are taking place in libraries today. In this age of computers we now have online bibliographic networks, turnkey library systems, online databases, microcomputers to support local library functions, computer output microform and, most recently, video disk and CD-ROM. But these wonderful new opportunities for extended access to information will create their own problems.

We are just beginning to understand the costs involved with these new information sources: equipment, information conversion, staff training, increased demand, telecommunication, and more.

New policy issues arise. Concern for access is beginning to replace the need for ownership. But then how do we decide who pays and how do we manage that growing world of information? These and other provocative questions challenge our thinking and force us to consider new options.

Patricia Battin, Vice President for Information Services and University Librarian, Columbia University, recently described the sort of librarian that will be needed in this period of transition to the 21st century. "The decade ahead of us will require individuals who are capable of managing the traditional labor intensive services, who also have the imagination and creativity to design new systems and who have the talent and skill to put them into place."[19]

At MIT the campus is linked through a powerful computer network, Project Athena, which integrates the libraries with the Institute's teaching mission in a way that may portend the future for many other libraries. Lucker describes the goals of Project Athena:

> Academic libraries have traditionally collected, organized, and made available information crucial to the educational process at their individual institutions. In recent years, libraries have increased the scope of their collections beyond the boundaries of traditional print sources, accelerated the use of electronic technologies in controlling and delivering their resources, taken a broadened view of themselves as interdependent members of a national and international resource, as opposed to isolated, self-sufficient institutions, and provided programs of innovative services to their users.
>
> The results of the implementation of this project will be a permanent change and improvement in the information gathering work of MIT students, faculty, and researchers. Information now housed in a multitude of locations and available during limited hours will be available as universally in space and time as Athena terminals. The benefits of sophisticated information storage and retrieval mechanisms will become available to MIT students, whether within or outside the walls of the libraries.[20]

In the 2 years since that paper was given, other technologies are making information more available. The libraries at MIT, working with the School of Architecture, have mastered an optical disk. They are now working together on a database with a videodisk of slides of Boston Architecture, which is planned for transmission across the campus.

At the Columbia University Libraries, the Pew foundation is supporting a program to test the impact of CD-ROM on instruction and research. Among the several creative projects that are planned is the creation of a Write Once Read Many (WORM) optical disk database of bibliographic, numeric, textual, and graphic geophysical data. This project will be done in cooperation with the library by scientists at the Lamont-Doherty Geological Observatory. Like other programs of this type, it is a monumental undertaking that attempts to reify the ideal of the library as part of the concept of the Scholarly Information Center.

Another project, code name APOLLO, to speed access to scientific information in the European Community, is being tested at the British Lending Library. It is a satellite-based delivery system which uses a high speed digital transmission channel to send documents from supply centers to users. Documents will be received much more quickly and with much higher resolution than in previous facsimile transmission.[21]

Maintaining collections and databases, making information accessible to researchers, planning for growth, finding ways to pay for it all: these have been concerns of science librarians in the 19th and 20th centuries. Librarians in these last few years of the 20th century must deal with these problems while planning for the exciting options for the future. As the latest generation of pioneers, we will look forward to using the evolving technology to increase access beyond the walls of the library and to enable our users to find information in its many forms. As Melvil Dewey said a century ago:

> These are the facts. The old library was passive, asleep, a reservoir or cistern, *getting* in but not giving out, an arsenal in time of peace; the librarian a sentinel before the doors, a jailer to guard against the escape of the unfortunates under his care. The new library is active, an aggressive, educating force in the community, . . . an army in the field with all guns limbered; and the librarian occupies a field of active usefulness second to none.[22]

I think he might look at our new vision and be pleased.

REFERENCES

1. Dewey, Melvil. Library as related to the educational work of the state. *In*: Vann, Sarah, ed. *Melvil Dewey: his enduring presence in librarianship*. Littleton, Colorado: Libraries Unlimited; 1978; p. 136. Harris, Michael H., gen. ed. *The heritage of librarianship series; no. 4*.

2. Farlow, W.G. Memoir of Asa Gray. National Academy of Sciences. *Biographical Memoirs. III*. Washington, D.C.: National Academy of Sciences; 1895: p. 161-175.

3. Farlow, W.G. p. 165.

4. Love, James Lee. *The Lawrence Scientific School in Harvard University*. 1847-1900. Burlington, N.C.: 1944.

5. Lyon, Jr., Marcus Ward. Father Nieuwland the botanist. *The catalyzer*. The Julius Arthur Nieuwland Memorial Edition. 42-44; 1937 February.

6. Laboratory and pharmaceutical sales department. Corning Glass Works. *Famous names in chemical history. Father Nieuwland*. Corning Glass Works; Corning, N.Y.; 1948; p. 3-25.

7. Havlik, Robert J. *Father Julius A. Nieuwland and the 50th anniversary of neoprene*. South Bend, I.N. Unpublished paper. 1981.

8. Schlereth, Thomas J. *The University of Notre Dame*. South Bend, IN: University of Notre Dame Press; 1976.

9. Hansen, Ralph W. Stanford University Libraries. *In*: Kent, Allen; Lancour Harold. *Encyclopedia of Library and Information Science*. New York: Marcel Dekker; 1968; Vol. 29, p. 17-18.

10. *Massachusetts Institute of Technology, Boston. A brief account of its foundation, character, and equipment*. Boston: Massachusetts Institute of Technology; 1983: p. 17.

11. Bigelow, Robert Payne. Librarian, 1895 to 1925. *Early days in the M.I.T. Library*. Unpublished paper from the Institute Archives and Special Collections, MIT Libraries, Cambridge, Mass.

12. *Massachusetts Institute of Technology, Boston*. p. 17.

13. Peterson, Kenneth G. *The University of California Library at Berkeley*. 1900-1945. Berkeley: University of California Press; 1970: p. 141.

14. Peterson, Kenneth G. p. 141-142.

15. Dewey, Melvil. Our next half-century. Vann, Sarah. p. 219.

16. Nicholson, Natalie N. Massachusetts Institute of Technology Libraries. *In*: Kent, Allen; Lancour, Harold. Vol. 17. p. 241.

17. Tarbell, Arthur Wilson. *The story of Carnegie Tech: being a history of Carnegie Institute of Technology from 1900 to 1935*. Pittsburgh: Carnegie Institute of Technology; 1937: p. 149-150.

18. Lucker, Jay K. Technological advances and the changing research library—from yesterday to tomorrow. Koskiala, Sinikka; Fjallbrant, Nancy, eds. Library development: North America: *Proceedings of the IATUL: International Association of Technological University Libraries; 1985*. Goteburg, Sweden: IATUL; 18;1986.

19. Battin, Patricia. Columbia University Libraries. *Challenge for the next ten years*. Paper presented to the Columbia University, Administrative Budget Committee, February 1987.

20. Lucker, Jay K. p. 25.

21. APOLLO. Document delivery enters the space age. *British Library News*. 122: 2; 1987 February.

22. Dewey, Melvil. Libraries as related to the educational work of the state. Vann, Sarah. p. 131.

Science and Technology Departments in Public Libraries: A Review of the Past Century

Jean Z. Piety
Evelyn M. Ward

SUMMARY. Public libraries in the United States had their origins in New England during the late eighteenth century. By 1876, the significant developments included the first meeting of a professional association, and the introduction of Melvil Dewey's classification scheme. By the turn of the century, technical information was increasing and the public need for access to it led to the development of science and technology departments in public libraries. New York, Pittsburgh, Cleveland, and Detroit were among the first large public libraries to establish such departments. A unique arrangement in Chicago was an early resource-sharing project. Significant events after World War II included the establishment of the Linda Hall Library and the rise of the environmental movement. Automation, interlibrary cooperation, and continuing increases in technical publication will be prominent features on the landscape of the future as science and technology departments respond to the challenge of providing timely access to the right information.

THE BEGINNINGS

History of Urban Public Libraries

The history of the public library in the United States is interwoven with the social history of the country, and that social history is studded with the achievements of individuals having distinctive tastes and interests, men like Andrew Carnegie and John Crerar.

Jean Z. Piety is the Head of the Science and Technology Department, and Evelyn M. Ward is Head of the Literature Department, both at the Cleveland Public Library, 325 Superior Avenue, Cleveland, OH 44114-1271.

© 1988 by The Haworth Press, Inc. All rights reserved.

The philanthropy of these men laid the foundation for the existence of libraries and their role in serving the public.

To define precisely what is a public library would be an essay in itself. Jesse Shera's chapter on the beginnings of the public library quotes from the 1876 Report of the U.S. Bureau of Education by William F. Poole: 'The public library' which we are to consider is established by state laws, is supported by local taxation or voluntary gifts, is managed as a public trust, and every citizen of the city or town which maintains it has an equal share in its privileges of reference and circulation."[1]

A recent article credits Benjamin Franklin with creating the first public library in this country in 1790 in Franklin, Massachusetts. When approached by the town officials with the suggestion that he donate a bell for the town steeple, Franklin responded with a gift of a library, saying that "sense is preferable to sound."[2] The fact that the town officials took 2 more years to decide who should be allowed to read these books, and the fact that the books themselves languished in a hay loft for even more years,[3] suggests the difficulties of attempting to define the public library.

Similar tales can be told of other communities throughout New England, as subscription libraries, social libraries, and circulating libraries came into existence. Many of these later became the public libraries of their towns, and were supported by municipal funds. As New England developed and became more populated, there was a determined group who had a desire for knowledge and perceived a need for libraries.

Paradoxically, what might be described as the first step on the road toward science and technology subject departments in public libraries was a move to consolidate rather than divide. On February 2, 1826, George Ticknor, as a trustee of the Boston Athenaeum, proposed that all the libraries of Boston be united. In a letter to Daniel Webster, he described his plan to unite the various libraries, such as the Architectural Library, the Medical Library, and the new Scientific Library, into one establishment, and then to let the whole circulate, including the holdings of the Athenaeum. Thus, he argued, duplication in buying, renting, and staffing would be avoided.[4] Ticknor then assumed leadership in the movement to establish the Boston Public Library, and began by collecting lists of essential books from every interested scholar. The efforts of Ticknor and others culminated in the establishment of Boston as the first large urban public library, which opened its reading room on March 20, 1854, at the Adams schoolhouse in Mason Street.

The Events of 1876

By 1870, the U.S. Commissioner of Education reported that, of the 209 librarians in the United States, 99 were in Massachusetts and New York.[5] By 1876, there were 188 public libraries in 11 states, ranging from 127 in Massachusetts to 1 each in Iowa and Texas. As public libraries developed, so did a concern for solving mutual problems. Melvil Dewey, the young managing editor of the new *American Library Journal*, issued a call for a convention of librarians. Held during the Centennial Exposition in Philadelphia in 1876, the Convention attracted 103 attendees, and thus the American Library Association was born.

At the same time, Dewey described his new method of classification, which he had applied to the Amherst College Library collection. His notion was to divide all of printed knowledge into 10 subject areas, which would then be further subdivided into classes. This scheme created the framework which later made it possible for large urban libraries to organize their main library collections into subject departments.

The Open Shelf Arrangement

As urban areas developed, so did libraries for the public. Industries drew more people to the cities. By 1890, Cleveland, Ohio, was 10th in the rank of American cities, with a population of 261,353, an increase of more than 600% over 1860. Cincinnati held 8th place and Detroit's population was steadily climbing.[6] Factories and mills were multiplying in all 3 cities, drawing workers from many different nationalities. Library needs were no longer limited to the scholar and the bookworm.

At the time, the Cleveland Library's director was William Howard Brett, a man who was not only receptive to new ideas, but courageous in putting many of them into action.[7] The open shelf was one of those new ideas. From his own background in bookstores, he understood the value of direct handling of books. By putting books on open shelves, he helped to make the Library a vital part of the community. The immigrant could find titles that helped him to master English and the inventor could find diagrams that helped him to tinker.[8] Circulation figures proved the success of the open shelf in spite of the skeptics.

THE TURN OF THE CENTURY

The Rise of Technology

The turn of the century was a watershed for science and much of technology. The nineteenth century had ended with a whole range of new scientific breakthroughs. The framework of the Scientific Revolution of the seventeenth century was giving way to fields of investigation that were not explicable in simple terms. That classic set, *History of Technology*, covered the period from the dawn of civilization to the end of the nineteenth century in five volumes, yet it took two more volumes to review the technology of the first 50 years of the twentieth century. As Trevor Williams stated, the United States had "not only established a commanding position in traditional industries, such as iron and steel, but was a pioneer in wholly new industries, such as the manufacture of motor cars and aeroplanes."[9]

The Rise of Technical Indexes

As technology developed, so did the printed word. Not only did a significant number of new serials and periodicals arise, especially in engineering, but there was an increase in patent literature. The need for indexes was apparent. William Poole had already issued his *Index to Periodical Literature*. William Brett asked his staff to make a slip index of the "better" magazines. He persuaded the trustees to allow him to publish the compilation and offer a subscription to a *Cumulative Index to a Selected List of Periodicals*. This venture faltered after a few years, but was reviewed by Halsey W. Wilson, who merged it with his *Readers Guide to Periodical Literature*.[10] By 1913, H. W. Wilson realized the need for a more technical index and began publishing the *Industrial Arts Index*.

The Engineering Societies Library

Proceedings and transactions of professional engineering meetings were being published and maintained by several societies. There existed, in New York City, four important engineering societies: American Society of Civil Engineers, American Institute of Mining Engineers, American Society of Mechanical Engineers, and American Institute of Electrical Engineers. Each had mandates to preserve its publications. Although discussions favoring a joint library and headquarters building had been taking place, it was not until 1904 that the United Engineering Societies (UES) was formed.

The history of UES and the relationship of its library to *Engineering Index* is thoroughly documented in Ellis Mount's definitive book: *Ahead of its time*.[11] *Engineering Index* began modestly in October 1984 as index notes published in the *Journal* of the Association of Engineering Societies. Later, cumulative volumes were published covering 1884-91, 1892-95, 1896-1900, 1901-05, these being the first issues of *Engineering Index*. By 1905, the index was citing about 10,000 articles per year.[12] A brochure published by the UES as its building was nearing completion in 1907 featured the library, which almost immediately became known informally as the "Engineering Societies Library," a name formally adopted in 1918. That brochure quoted the trustees in hopes that all organizations who were to be welcomed to the building would add their libraries, so that this library might become one of the notables of the world. "It is to be conducted as a free library of reference."[13]

Major Urban Libraries

Other mergers were occurring in New York City at the same time. The Astor Library, which had opened in 1854, had been designed as a free reference library, but, without electricity, had very short hours. The Lenox Library, opened in 1877, was restricted in its collections for public use.[14] In the 1890s, the trustees of the Samuel J. Tilden estate decided that the money from the estate would be used to create a public library. A consolidation of these three led to the establishment of the New York Public Library at Fifth Avenue and 42nd Street.

When the building opened in 1911, the Technology and Patent

Division comprised materials gathered from the Astor and Lenox libraries. The Director of the Library, Dr. John Shaw Billings, and the Division head, William Gamble, selected the materials for the new division as well as the technical books for both the central circulating unit and the library's branches. Dr. Billings had built the Surgeon General's Library in Washington.[15]

Mr. Gamble described his division as "five magnificent rooms on the main floor of the new central building." The collection, which included the engineering books from the Astor Library, was definitely a research library:

> In small degree only does it correspond to the "Useful Arts room" as ordinarily understood. The boy who desires to make a wireless outfit for $3, or the fireman who would "bone up" for a civil service examination through the help of a locomotive catechism, is directed elsewhere. The division is intended for the man who would "get at the bottom of things" the engineer, the inventor, the manufacturer.[16]

He went on to say that books written in the popular style could be requisitioned from the central circulation room, conveniently located nearby. He hoped to have a card catalog soon, and to have the index cards to the engineering periodical articles available. Although, by terms of the Astor will, no material could circulate, the division was open to any serious applicant who would "take the trouble to sign the register."[17]

The Science Division received the same care in selection of materials and opened with 4,800 monographs, while the Technology and Patent Division started with 5,000. The two sections remained separate until 1919, when they were combined to become the Science and Technology Division.[18]

An earlier effort to serve the public by means of a specialized science and technology department had been initiated farther west. Just as the UES building would not have been possible without the financial assistance of Andrew Carnegie, the city of Pittsburgh also benefited from Carnegie's early philanthropies. The Carnegie Library of Pittsburgh was opened in 1895, with a collection of 16,000 volumes available to the public. The librarian's annual report included a plea for the money to establish a strong technical collection. By 1897, Pittsburgh was a major industrial city and, in that year alone, the library served 270,000 people, a number equal to the city's population. By 1902, the library opened its Science/technology service, and thus became the first public library to have a separate subject department for science and technology.[19]

The first decade of the twentieth century saw several urban libraries develop subject departments in their main buildings. The perceived need for a subject arrangement seemed to be closely related to the increasing importance of technology in the lives of people at many levels of society. These developments, combined with the enormous growth in publication, encouraged public libraries to organize by subject. Although classification schemes like the Dewey Decimal system existed, the question of what to include in subject departments and what to call the science/technology ones continued to plague administrators. An editorial in the supplement to *Engineering News* for December 12, 1907, dealt with the dilemma of technical works in public libraries:

> Outside of the collection of a few technical societies and schools, the attention paid by libraries to scientific books is far below that required by their importance. When the average engineer has need for study out of the ordinary line of his work, the necessary limitations of his own library, consisting probably of the standard works of the profession with a few extra treatises on his own specialties, force him to have recourse to the public library. There usually the insatiable demand for popular fiction makes such a drain upon the funds of the institution and the time of its employees that the few technical books which are on the shelves are poorly classified and hard to locate.

That editorial prompted N. D. C. Hodges, Librarian at the Public Library in Cincinnati, Ohio, to respond in the issue of January 16, 1908:

> Sir: My attention was called this morning to the editorial in your issue of Dec. 12 on technical works in public libraries, and it occurred to me that your readers might be interested in knowing that a special room was set aside in the main building of this library as a useful arts room in March, 1902. In this room we have the recent books on applied science to the number of three or four thousand, and there are kept on file 260 periodicals, these mainly on applied science. Our useful arts room is visited each day by 300 persons, most of them men; these are the manufacturers and experts, engineers, chemists, and electricians, and last, but not least, the artisans. Cincinnati is a manufacturing city, and it has been our attempt for the past five years and more to make this department serviceable to such a city. As a bureau of information in applied science, with back of it a great storehouse of bound scientific periodicals and the older books containing such information, it seems probable that this department repays all that the public library costs.[20]

Cincinnati called its science department a useful arts room, while others chose different terms. An Industrial Library at the Providence Public Library opened in 1900; a Technical Department at the Newark Public Library in 1908; an Applied Science Department at the St. Louis Public Library in 1910; an Applied Science Reference Room in Brooklyn in 1905; and a Useful Arts Department in Minneapolis in 1910. Pratt Institute Free Library, in 1904, offered current journals of different trades, together with engineering journals and reference books that were being acquired, and was also developing a collection of trade catalogs.[21]

In the Midwest, collection building in the technical field continued. In 1896, Detroit Public Library acquired its first book on the automobile, thus laying the foundation for the Automotive History Collection. The book was John Henry Knight's *Notes on Motor Carriages with Hints for Purchasers and Users*. The author counseled prospective buyers "to see the machine taken to pieces and put together again before purchasing." The preface to the published catalog of the collection read like the development of the automobile itself. Some companies existed long enough to publish some literature about their machines, and the advertisements for autos have become jewels in the form of brochures, catalogs, and folders.[22]

The Technology Department of the Detroit Public Library started in 1917, but it was much later that the Automotive History Collection was formally recognized as a special collection. Charles Mohrhardt, who was Chief of the Technology Department in the 1930s, found that materials on the automobile and the industry existed in the library, but were not organized into a collection. It was not until he was associate librarian and Ralph A. Ulveling was director that they were able to make the collection an important one. In 1944, the Automotive History Collection formally came into existence; in 1953, it received divisional status under the Technology and Science Department. Today the Collection is of inestimable value to historians, technicians, commercial artists, and those seeking data for the restoration of vintage cars.[23] The published catalog serves as a valuable reference tool in many libraries.

Industry in the Midwest centered around the automobile. Cleveland was the hub of automobile and automotive parts manufacturing, with firms like Winton, Jordan, and Baker Electric. By 1913, the Cleveland Public Library had deposit collections in 14 factories, 3 department stores, and 11 telephone exchanges. The Main Library was being reorganized into subject departments, but service to the public from a departmentalized arrangement could not begin until September of 1913. The move of the Main Library to the sixth floor of the Kinney & Levan Building at Thirteenth and Euclid Avenue provided the opportunity to carry out the plan of dividing the reference collection into subject departments.[24]

The Technology Division opened in 1913 with subjects in the natural sciences and useful arts, except for domestic science, which was relegated to the Popular Library." (This division of materials was tried again when the Business and Technology Department moved into its new building in 1959, but again proved unsuccessful.) Mr. Gilbert Ward, Head of the division, stated in his first annual report that the needs were "additional shelving for the circulating books, and increased seating capacity for readers."[26] He also reported that the periodicals were now classed with the related literature, and that the patents had been brought out of storage and were easily available to the reader. Both the classing of periodicals and the housing of United States patents were to change under later administrations.

In 1915, Carl Vitz, as the second vice librarian in charge of the Main Library, described the physical layout and the problems encountered in the "Cleveland experiment with departmentalized reference work."[27] The current quarters were temporary, but the experience would help in planning the permanent layout. He believed that staff had suffered because no card catalog had been easily available in the early years. He reported that the critics claimed there were difficulties created because the staff did not have a total picture of all the resources. On the other hand, the creation of the subject specialist, who knew his collection better than the generalist, gave service to the patron in a better fashion.

Today two buildings form the nucleus for public service. Besides the Main Library that opened in 1925, the Business and Science Building was acquired through a bond issue in 1958. Opened for service in August 1959, this building was designed to serve the business and technical community. What was called the Business and Technology Department in 1959 has now become two very active subject departments, the Business, Economics and Labor Department, and the Science and Technology Department. With the separation of federal documents from the subject departments in 1975, the third department in the same building is the Documents Collection.

The John Crerar Library

While the major urban public libraries were recognizing the need for service to specific client groups, a unique arrangement was appearing in Chicago. John Crerar, one of Chicago's leading businessmen, provided in his will for a free Public library to be located in the City of Chicago. His 1894 will stipulated that books and periodicals were

> to be selected with a view to create and sustain a wealthy moral and Christian sentiment in the community and that all nastiness and immorality be excluded, that dirty French novels

and all skeptical trash and works of questionable moral tone shall never be found in this library.[28]

Chicago Public Library had been flourishing since 1873 and the Newberry Library since 1888. The John Crerar Library was incorporated on October 12, 1894.[29] The directors of these institutions soon began to consider balancing and coordinating their respective functions. By 1895, the plan was that the Public Library include

> all wholesomely entertaining and generally instructive books, especially such as are desired by the citizens for general home use. Also, collections of newspapers, patents, government documents, books for the blind, and in architecture and the decorative arts.[30]

The Newberry was to continue buying in literature, language, history, sociology, philosophy, physical and natural sciences, the useful arts (technology), the fine arts in part, sociology, and economics. The plan changed through the years, notably when Crerar took over coverage of medicine from Newberry and gave up buying in the social sciences.[31] The cooperation of these three libraries in establishing the goals of their collections serves as an early example of urban library resource-sharing.

Originally housed in Chicago's loop, the John Crerar Library moved into its own quarters in 1920, across from the Chicago Public Library. By 1962, although centrally located, these facilities became seriously overcrowded. An agreement with the Illinois Institute of Technology was made and the library moved to that campus. That arrangement was terminated by both parties in 1980. A new contract in 1981 between the University of Chicago and the Crerar Board culminated in locating the Crerar Library in a new building on the University of Chicago campus.[32] Patricia Swanson, who directs the new John Crerar Library, stated that "a merger of this size and complexity is unprecedented in American research library history."[33] Throughout all these changes the public continued to have access to the collection, as stipulated under John Crerar's will.

Thus, urban public libraries were recognizing the need for specialized reference work by having subject departments or special collections for specific client groups whose interests had, in the previous century, been met by the mercantile and apprentices' libraries. Carnegie's money and the need for space formed a combination that resulted in the construction of several large urban central library buildings in the 1920s.

In the thirties, the rise in unemployment brought an increase in calls for material on vocational subjects. As the libraries recovered from the Depression, World War II began. Although World War I had slowed the development of library services, this was not true during World War II. There were book drives, and large public libraries became Defense Information Clearinghouses, with information on victory gardens, rationing, and draft boards, and even classes in defense training. A need for technical manuals became apparent, as people taking new defense jobs in industry required practical, well-illustrated, up-to-date guides.[34]

AFTER WORLD WAR II

The Linda Hall Library

After the war, another public library that serves the science community was founded in Kansas City, Missouri. When Henry Hall died in 1941, his bequest provided a trust fund of six million dollars to establish "a free public library for the use of the people of Kansas City and the public generally." The will stipulated that the library was to be located on the Hall grounds and that it was to be named after Mr. Hall's wife, Linda, who had died in 1938.[35] Four consultants independently agreed that the need was for a research library in the science and technology field. Accepting this recommendation, the trustees hired Joseph Shipman as the first librarian, who served from 1945 until his retirement in 1973. In 1946, the Linda Hall Library opened in the family mansion. When the trustees bought the library collection of the American Academy of Arts and Sciences in Boston, the library acquired retrospective holdings rich in scientific journals and historically significant monographs. This collection, and the staff's concentration on acquiring other serial runs, formed the basis of the Library's current acquisitions policy and its strong position in the science world today. Mr. Peterson, now the Administrative Assistant at Linda Hall, in describing the library, stated that it "has one of the most extensive scientific and technical collections anywhere."[36] Mr. Shipman anticipated that a service of the Library would be "to provide a list of periodicals subscribed to which can be widely distributed in this area."[37] That list, now the bible in the science field, is used for identifying serial titles.

Considered a reference library, Linda Hall does not circulate its books, but does lend, outside the metropolitan area, through regular interlibrary loan arrangements. By 1978, serials accounted for 90% of all requests received, so the library policy on lending was modified to exclude conferences and proceedings. Today the Library is noted throughout the science community for its photocopy services. The current and third director, Larry Besant, wants "to increase accessibility of Linda Hall Library's outstanding scientific and technical store of materials by participating in . . . networks . . ."[38]

The Environmental Movement

By the 1960s, environmentalists were becoming concerned over certain effects of the technological advances made in this century. In the library world, of all the fields of knowledge that were part of the information explosion, environmental studies did not fit neatly into any classification scheme. Patrons had to use several departments to obtain material on conservation or on environmental issues. Some libraries started to recognize the public's frustrations. The Conservation Library of the Denver Public Library was established in 1960 under the guidance of John T. Eastlick and writer/conservationist Arthur Carhart. Up to this time, there was no one collection in a public library devoted to conservation.[39]

Although the scope of the Denver Conservation Collection included all aspects of environmental studies, it was not until the early seventies that the key term became "environment." Sigurd F. Olson was active in establishing an environmental library for Minnesotans. When ECOL was launched as part of the Minneapolis Public Library during Earth Week of 1972, Mr. Olson summarized the underlying philosophy of the collection: "wisdom is what this environmental library is all about — the dissemination of wisdom so that we can meet these battles intelligently, and with a possible chance of winning . . . If we save the earth and its beauties, man's spirit will survive."[40]

Projects like these two existed only through the initiative and drive of individuals like Mr. Carhart and Mr. Olson. In 1973 in Cleveland, the George Gund Foundation aided in transforming the Environmental Island in the Science and Technology Department into the Environmental Resources Center. The Foundation gave the library an opportunity to help inform the public on environmental concerns and a chance to strengthen the resources in the library. When the funding for the project ceased in 1979, the resources augmented several subject departments, including the Science and Technology Department.

Toward the Twenty-First Century

The keys to the next century will be cooperation, online capabilities, networking, and document delivery. No one science and technology department can house everything.

The information explosion has continued to plague science and technology staff who are trying to give service and administrators who need to find ways to store knowledge. Those who worked with the Atomic Energy Commission documents realized what a space saving there was when these documents were issued on microfiche. The microfilm of the United States Patents is an even more impressive space saver. Today the proliferation of information is making it more and more difficult, if not impossible, to create or maintain a complete resource library. On the eve of receiving the first volume of the *Eleventh Collective Index to Chemical Abstracts*, one is preoccupied with finding room to house the entire set, which represents an enormous increase in size when compared with the first cumulation of 1907-1916. Similar comparisons could be made between the first cumulation and the current one for *Science Citation Index*. A tabulation of the number of early titles in Bowker's *Pure & Applied Science Books, 1876-1982* shows how book publishing has paralleled the information explosion.[41]

In the Cleveland Public Library in the 1970s, the administrative decision to separate federal documents and microform formats from the subject departments provided for a more balanced work load among the staff. Separating the federal technical documents from the Science and Technology Department enabled the staff to concentrate on other aspects of the collection, such as expanding the standards collection. Referring the patron to Documents Collection may be more difficult for the patron to grasp initially, but, with perseverance, balanced service can be given.

Online services are performing an increasingly important role in literature searches and in routine reference work. Some libraries, like Boston Public's Science and Technology Department, routinely search online and charge back the computer costs to the patron. Others use Dialog for quick reference work. Dialog experimented with public libraries in the early 1970s, starting with libraries that could bill back to the patron.[42] Today online searches are even simpler through the use of microcomputers.

Cooperative efforts exist to aid staff in referral questions and in document delivery. Libraries, like New York Public Library, Linda Hall, Engineering Societies Library, and Cleveland Public's Science and Technology Department, provide photocopy services that reach out worldwide. Dialog's "Yellow Pages" form a directory of sources for information retrieval. The *Chemical Abstracts Service Source Index* is both a bibliographic tool and a source of holding libraries.

The plans developed by the John Crerar Library, Chicago Public Library, and the Newberry Library at the turn of the century were an unusual example of early library cooperation. Today the computer puts information closer to the patron in cooperative ways like the OCLC database, in joint cataloging efforts, and in realization that no one library can be everything to everyone. The key to public service will continue to be the ability to retrieve the right information at the right time.

REFERENCES

1. Shera, Jesse Hauk. *Foundations of the public library; the origins of the public library movement in New England, 1629-1855.* Chicago: University of Chicago Press; 1949: p. 157.

2. Baughman, James C. Sense is preferable to sound. *Library Journal.* 111(17): 42-44; 1986 October 15.

3. Shera., op. cit., p. 205.

4. Ibid., p. 207.

5. Garrison, Dee. *Apostles of culture: the public librarian and American society, 1876-1920*. New York: The Free Press; 1979: p. 3-4.

6. Rose, William Ganson. *Cleveland: the making of a city*. Cleveland: The World Publishing Company; 1950: p. 500.

7. Cramer, C. H. *Open shelves and open minds: a history of the Cleveland Public Library*. Cleveland: The Press of Case Western Reserve University; 1972: p. 49.

8. Rose., op. cit., p. 508.

9. Williams, Trevor I. *A short history of twentieth century technology: c. 1900- c. 1950*. New York: Oxford University Press; 1982: p. 2.

10. Cramer., op. cit., p. 60.

11. Mount, Ellis. *Ahead of its time: the Engineering Societies Library, 1913-80*. Hamden, Ct: Linnet Books; 1982.

12. Ibid., p. 163.

13. Ibid., p. 60.

14. Ibid., p. 30.

15. Ibid., p. 32.

16. Gamble, William B. Technology and patent divisions of the New York Public Library. *Library Journal*. 36(12): 634-635. 1911 December.

17. Ibid., p. 635.

18. Dain, Phyllis. *The New York Public Library: a history of its founding and early years*. New York: New York Public Library; 1972: p. 328.

19. Mount., op. cit., p. 38.

20. Technical works in public libraries. *Public Libraries* 13:87, 1908 March.

21. Kruzas, Anthony Thomas. *Business and industrial libraries in the United States, 1820-1940*. New York: Special Libraries Association; 1965: p. 34.

22. *The automotive history collection of the Detroit Public Library: a simplified guide to its holdings*. Boston: G. K. Hall & Co.; 1966.

23. Woodford Frank Bury. *Parnassus on Main Street: a history of the Detroit Public Library*. Detroit: Wayne State University Press; 1965: p. 342.

24. Cleveland Public Library Board. *Forty-fifth annual report for the year 1913*. Cleveland: Lezius Printing Co.

25. Ward, Gilbert O. ibid., p. 62.

26. Ibid., p. 63.

27. Vitz, Carl. Cleveland experience with departmentalized reference work. *American Library Association Bulletin*. 9:169-174; 1915 May.

28. John Crerar Library. *The John Crerar Library: 1885-1944*. Chicago; 1945: p. 24.

29. Ibid., p. 30.

30. Ibid., p. 29.

31. Mount., op. cit., p. 37.

32. Swanson, Patricia K. The John Crerar Library of the University of Chicago. *Science & Technology Libraries*. 7(1): 3043; 1986 Fall.

33. Ibid., p. 32.

34. Epstein, Jacob S. History of urban main library service. *Library Trends.* 20:598-624; 1972 April.

35. Peterson, Paul. In full bloom: Linda Hall Library. *Wilson Library Bulletin.* 57(2):122-127; 1982 October: (p. 123).

36. Ibid., p. 122.

37. Shipman, Joseph C. Linda Hall Library. *Library Journal* 71:1587-90; 1946 November 15: (p. 1590).

38. Peterson., op. cit., p. 127.

39. Denver Public Library. *Catalog of the Conservation Library.* Boston: G. K. Hall & Co.; 1974: p. iii.

40. Sigurd F. Olson and ECOL. *ECOL News* 6(2):1. 1982 February.

41. *Pure & applied science books, 1876-1982.* New York: R. R. Bowker; 1982: p. vii.

42. Summit, Roger K; Firschein, Oscar. *Investigation of the public library as a linking agent to major scientific, educational, social, and environmental data bases: final report.* Palo Alto, CA: Information Systems Programs, Lockheed Missiles and Space Company, Inc.; 1977 October 1; LMSC-D560986-vi. 175p. Available from: NTIS PB276726.

Scientific and Technical Libraries in the Federal Government: One Hundred Years of Service

Sarah Thomas Kadec
Carol B. Watts

SUMMARY. Following a review of publications that examine various aspects of government libraries, the authors trace the history of the founding and development of federal libraries. Future trends for such libraries are also discussed.

INTRODUCTION

Scientific and technical libraries have been an important part of the federal library scene, almost since the beginning of the development of federal libraries. These libraries could, should, and would play an important role in the process of advancing the national policy and goals through strong, effective, and responsive government, and through technological advances, which would bring about a high level of development, growth, and standard of living to the nation.

As government changes and reorganizes, and as national priorities change, libraries in the federal government experience ups and

---

Sarah Thomas Kadec received an MLS degree from Carnegie Library School, Carnegie Institute of Technology. She retired from the U.S. Environmental Protection Agency as Deputy Director, Office of Information Resources Management in 1985, and set up a consulting business shortly thereafter.

Carol B. Watts received the MLS degree from the School of Library Science, Florida State University. Before establishing the Washington Information Network, she was employed with Aspen Systems Corporation as Library Manager on the Housing and Urban Development Department contract.

© 1988 by The Haworth Press, Inc. All rights reserved.

downs, consistent somewhat with the concerns of the day, and particularly with economic stresses, objectives of specific administrations, and global and national problems. The World War II period saw an increase in interest in scientific and technical information, as did the years immediately following it. The technological advancements of the 1940s, through the beginnings of the space age, reflected an increased interest in research and information to support it, and thus enhanced the library's status as a means of acquiring and providing access to such information.

STUDIES

As federal libraries became more visible and their services were recognized as having importance to organizations within the government, statistics began to be collected, studies were conducted, and efforts were made to coordinate their activities for the total benefit of the government. The first report on federal libraries appeared as Chapter 10, "Libraries of the Federal Government" in *Public Libraries in the United States of America*, published in 1876 by the Department of the Interior. It was not until nearly a century later that another study of federal libraries appeared.

The National Science Foundation was given authority to study and coordinate a variety of information activities centered in other agencies. Several major studies were carried out from the period after World War II through the early 1960s in an effort to organize information resource centers and avoid duplication of effort among agencies. Even though these studies were not specific to libraries, they impacted the way libraries did business, i.e., handling of technical report literature.

In 1963, *Federal Departmental Libraries: a Summary Report of a Survey and Conference*, was published by the Brookings Institution. It stressed the need for clear library policy consistent with overall departmental and agency policies. Few federal libraries, with the exception of the national libraries, were considered research libraries. Particularly within scientific and technical agencies library activities were coordinated, specifically the National Aeronautics and Space Administration, the Department of Agriculture, and the Veterans Administration, though little coordination existed across department lines of major libraries, creating problems for users and resulting in duplication of personnel time, and money.

This 1963 conference also drew particular attention to the incompatible cataloging systems. Specifically cited were the Library of Congress, the National Library of Medicine, the National Agricultural Library, the Armed Service Technical Information Agency (later to become the Defense Documentation Center), the Atomic Energy Commission, the National Aeronautics and Space Administration—the majority of these having strong scientific and technical collections.

The report of this conference also pointed out that demands for scientific and technical information and library services were generally expenditures for research and development. Libraries in science agencies were believed to have better funding, partly because research funds financed some of their activities.

By this time, the Federal Council for Science and Technology had joined the National Science Foundation in promoting interagency cooperation in the areas of scientific and technical information. Several important reports, including the Baker, Crawford, and Weinberg reports, were issued during this time and, though not specific to libraries, their impact was felt in all federal information activities, as was the establishment of the Committee on Scientific and Technical Information (COSATI) in 1964. The Federal Library Committee (FLC) at the Library of Congress was established in 1965, due in part to the recommendations of the 1963 conference. It sought to coordinate the work of all the agencies' libraries and information centers, not just the sci-tech ones.

In 1968, the Federal Library Committee and the Office of Education's National Center for Education Statistics (NCES) sponsored a survey of federal libraries. The report of the study, entitled *Survey of Special Libraries Serving the Federal Government*, was published by the Department of Health, Education and Welfare. This was followed by a survey in 1971-72 sponsored by the Federal Library Committee and the U.S. Office of Education in which it was determined that 52% (or 986) of the respondents were representative of technical or special libraries. This study was issued by the Department of Health, Education and Welfare in 1975 as the *Survey of Federal Libraries*.

EARLY BEGINNINGS

Most scientific and technical libraries and information centers were begun to further the major programs of the departments and agencies they served. The country's early concerns with resources, surveying land in the interior and coastal areas, weather, and the military, resulted in the establishment of certain agencies or their predecessors.

Though not established primarily as scientific and technical libraries, many of the early libraries had significant collections of scientific and technical information. The Army library at the Military Academy, though formally established in 1812, contained materials on engineering and military technology of the time as early as 1777. The Library of Congress, established in 1800 and strengthened in 1815 by the purchase of Thomas Jefferson's extensive private library, had its collections further strengthened by the transfer of collections from the Smithsonian's International Exchange System established in 1860. Yet the Library of Congress's Science Division was not officially established until 1949.

Some of the early federal libraries were primarily scientific and technical collections. These included the Interior Department Library (1850), the Smithsonian (1953), the Agriculture Department Library (1862), the Geological Survey (1882). During this same period, administrative programs were needed to standardize weights and measures and to protect inventions. The National Bureau of Standards (1901) and the Patent and Trademark Office (1936) libraries were established to provide information in support of these programs.

The Surgeon General of the Army's Library had a few troublesome years (1860-70s), but survived to become the Army Medical Library, the Armed Forces Medical Library and, in 1956, the basis for the National Library of Medicine. Other health-related libraries developed in the Department of Health, Education and Welfare in the 1860s and 1880s (beginnings of the present National Institutes of Health library).

Between 1901 and 1941, very few new scientific and technical libraries came into being. One exception to this was the establishment of the now Naval Air Systems Command Library in 1920.

Burton Adkinson describes the first period of library and information center development as 1790-1942, when institutions were established to address the government's information needs.[1]

INCREASED DEVELOPMENT

The 1940s and 50s saw an increase in the development of scientific and technical libraries in the federal government. By the 1940s there was a shift from the creation and use of trade journals and monographs to technical reports emanating from the growth of laboratories for research. Large-scale military document acquisition programs developed during World War II, supplemented by the volumes of technical publications obtained from Germany, and later, Japan. Libraries in government and around the nation felt the impact of this influx of technical literature in a format which libraries were not accustomed to handling.

The development of military libraries, including the National Facilities Engineering Command (1941), the Naval Medical Research Institute and the Corps of Engineers (both 1942), the Naval Sea Systems Command (1943), the Naval Surface Weapons Center and Army Library in the Pentagon (both 1944), and the Office of Naval Research (1948), all reflected the research and other programs generated by the war effort. The establishment of the Los Alamos Scientific Laboratory Library (1943) and the Atomic Energy Commission (1948) also resulted from World War II and efforts to develop the atomic bomb.

The next significant period in the development of scientific and technical libraries began with the launching of Sputnik by the Russians in 1957. This event brought new emphasis to the need for scientific and technical information to support a national effort to put a man into space and to generally move the U.S. into a leadership position in this and other technical arenas. The National Aeronautics and Space Administration (NASA) was formed from the National Advisory Committee for Aeronautics (NACA) and, like the Atomic Energy Commission (AEC), was a popular agency with a timely mission. It was well-funded and brought strong talent, often contracted, which created advanced and impressive high-tech information systems and products and services. The libraries which served these agencies tended to form internal networks and coordinate library support.

The 1960s and the social concerns of this period brought about the development of the libraries in such agencies as the Food and Drug Administration (1965). It also created a number of information centers and clearinghouses, often including libraries, in very specialized medical and health areas.

The late 1960s and early 1970s saw a number of organizational changes which created agencies and departments with a clear social orientation, resulting from social concerns such as the environment and scarcity of energy resources, i.e., Housing and Urban Development, Transportation, Environmental Protection Agency (1971), and the National Oceanic and Atmosphere Administration. Yet these had a heavy requirement for scientific and technical information to support the social actions they were being asked to undertake. Most of these departments and agencies inherited libraries from the agencies which were brought together in the new organizational entity. To assure information support, they relied on their libraries, on specialized information centers, and in some instances, on formal and informal networks, both these operating within the agencies and departments and those operated by other libraries and information centers in the same, or related, subject areas.

DEPARTMENTAL LIBRARIES

Few, if any, of the departments within the federal government can be considered solely concerned with science and technology, though many, such as the Departments of Agriculture, Energy, Health and Human Services, Interior, and Transportation have heavy scientific and technical collections. In many instances, the libraries which serve these departments with scientific and technical information are located in various subunits of the departmental structure.

The Department of Agriculture houses the National Agricultural Library whose holdings are heavily scientific and technically oriented ranging from basic soils data to biology, and from chemistry to biotechnology. It is a part of the Science and Education Administration within the department. A Blue Ribbon Panel review in 1982 gave new focus to the library and resulted in increased resources for both departmental and national support. Soon after the review, the Food and Nutrition Information Center moved to the National Agricultural Library. The department's Forest Service also has an extensive library network serving the agency field libraries around the country and linked to the National Agricultural Library.

The Department of Commerce houses two of the major scientific and technical libraries within the federal departmental structure — the National Bureau of Standards and the Patent Office Libraries. In addition, its National Oceanic and Atmospheric Agency supports a number of libraries in its various locations, in many instances under a library service contract, and its data centers often include a library component.

The Defense Department has no central library which serves the entire department. Instead, it relies on the extensive collection and services provided by the Army Library. Several components of the department's top structure do have libraries, such as the Defense Advanced Research Projects Agency (DARPA), and the Defense Intelligence Agency (DIA). DARPA's library is primarily scientific and technical, while the DIA Library contains primarily that scientific and technical data gathered as a routine matter through intelligence operations. The Army, Navy, and Air Force components, as shown in an earlier section of this article, maintain a large number of highly specialized libraries and information centers, often created as a result of war efforts and the research required to support such efforts. These include, among others, the Naval Research Laboratory and the various Naval Command Libraries, the Air Force's Research and Development Command Libraries, and the Army Redstone Arsenal Library. The Army's Corps of Engineers has a network of libraries located at its District sites.

The Department of Energy inherited its major library structure from the former Atomic Energy Commission, including those supporting such national laboratories as Los Alamos, Argonne, and Oak Ridge. Its libraries benefit from the extensive information collection, processing, and retrieval capabilities of its Technical Information Service.

The Department of Health, Education and Welfare houses both the National Library of Medicine and the National Institutes of

Health (NIH) library. The NIH library supports the institute's internal intramural scientific and medical programs, while the National Library of Medicine serves the nation's medical information needs. The Department also has extensive libraries in the Food and Drug Administration and the Center for Disease Control in Atlanta, Georgia. Within the department, there are many information centers and clearinghouses specializing in specific medical and health related topics, such as alcohol and drug abuse, smoking, mental health, and arthritis. Many of these centers contain libraries to support the reference and research work required of them.

The Department of Interior's main library serves as the National Natural Resources Library, and coordinates a network of the department's other libraries. Among the most notable of its scientific and technical libraries is the U.S. Geological Survey.

INDEPENDENT AGENCIES

Of the independent agencies, the National Aeronautics and Space Administration (NASA), the Environmental Protection Agency (EPA), and the National Science Foundation (NSF) have the most notable scientific and technical libraries. The National Science Foundation supports the internal research and program review needs of the foundation.

The NASA headquarters library and those at its research centers maintain libraries in a coordinated network designed to provide maximum information to support the space research program. As is true with the DOE, these libraries gain access to much of their collections through the extensive collecting, processing, and data base programs of the NASA Scientific and Technical Information Facility (STIF) and its arrangements with the private American Institute for Aeronautics and Astronautics (AIAA).

The EPA established a system of headquarters, regional, and laboratory libraries early in its history, designating specially areas of support for the engineering, health, and regulatory requirements of the agency. The library system became the focal point for the agency's publications control and, through arrangements with the National Technical Information Service (NTIS), reports are processed into the NTIS data base and microform copies of the actual reports are distributed to each of the libraries in the system. The headquarters library is currently an integral part of the information resources management (IRM) program for the agency.

THE NATIONAL LIBRARIES

The National Library of Medicine (NLM) has legal authority to provide a national medical information network. Medical schools and health facilities, as well as other federal libraries, rely heavily on its extensive MEDLINE database, created not only through the library's own collecting but through international agreements with medical facilities around the world. The library maintains the TOXLINE system, a national medical audiovisual center, and training to facilitate the use of medical and health information throughout the nation. It cooperates with the Library of Congress and the National Agricultural Library in shared cataloging and other cooperative efforts.

The National Agricultural Library (NAL) serves the staff of the Department of Agriculture and at the same time provides numerous services to the land grant colleges and universities in the country. These universities benefit from the AGRICOLA database, from thesaurus efforts in its work with the Food and Agriculture Organization, and from specialized collections, some of which are now being converted to compact disks through its program to increase the use of technology in the provision of agricultural information.

The NAL, the NLM, and the Library of Congress's Science and Technology Division carry out extensive interlibrary loans to other government libraries, and have influenced these libraries in the way collections are processed and made available. Their positions among libraries have permitted them to move ahead in the use of technology and the setting of standards for descriptive and subject cataloging, from which the other libraries have benefited.

TRENDS IN FEDERAL SCIENTIFIC AND TECHNICAL LIBRARIES AND INFORMATION CENTERS

The Library of Congress was the first recognized and legislated federal library. Since then federal libraries have grown out of the necessities of governmental administration, beginning with a small collection of materials, added to as the demands for them grew. Most libraries had to clear policy governing acquisitions, services, or their role in support of the department or agency mission. Later, scientific and technical libraries, particularly those in the Department of Defense, enunciated acquisition policies to control the range of materials to be collected. A task force on a library mission did arrive at a federal library mission statement and presented it to the Federal Library and Information Center Committee. It was approved by the administrative officers of the Executive Branch agencies in October 1966, with the assistance of the Office of Management and Budget. This however, was a statement of principles and guidelines and not an overall policy statement, and today scientific and technical libraries operate without a consistent policy from agency to agency.

Exchanges have strengthened the collections of federal scientific and technical libraries, individually or through the assistance of the Smithsonian Institution. Individual agencies have often arranged exchange agreements with universities carrying out research in their subject area, with private industrial research organizations, and often with other governmental agencies worldwide, again in the specific subject area of concern. Today, these exchange agreements are in danger due to the budget constraints faced by many of the participating organizations. User charges have become commonplace, particularly in instances where the exchanges may appear to benefit one of the organizations more than the other. Charges for government information have become more commonplace as agencies, such as NLM, charge for access to information. The emphasis placed on self-supporting operations will continue and will strain existing exchange relationships even more, and libraries are likely to begin instituting user charges for services other than photocopy and interlibrary loans, including reference and research services.

World War II, the space age, and intense social concerns have all brought about an increase in scientific and technical libraries over the last 50 years. Budgetary constraints and the current concern over the value, and hence, the costs of information are likely to lead to decreases in the number of existing libraries rather than an increase, despite the urgency of the issues at hand. There may well be some fallout for technical information activities from the present strategic defense initiative (SDI), but this will be limited compared to the developments experienced in the 1940—early 1970 time period. Information activities which do develop will certainly be around more limited subject areas of concern, where the size of the information base can be expected to have limitations, both in size and costs. This may account for the emergence of new clearinghouses over the past year or two.

Though a general reduction of R&D support for libraries and information centers has continued into the 1980s, there are indications that research and development budgets may increase slightly over the next few years to offset gains being made by other industrialized nations, cracks which appear to be developing in some of the major scientific and technical programs (i.e., space) and the trade imbalance of today. These increases in funds, if realized, will eventually filter down to the scientific and technical libraries which support the research organizations. Such support will be gradual and not a windfall, which many feel is needed to bring federal libraries back to the prominence they have had during some periods in history. Much of the funding may well be directed to more specialized information centers which will be staffed with people familiar with library and information center procedures as well as scientific and technical subject matter.

The Federal Library and Information Center Committee has achieved a place of importance among all federal libraries, including scientific and technical ones. It has developed, for federal libraries and other federal entities, coordinated approaches to cataloging, serials acquisitions and control, technology applications, and access to databases maintained by various vendors. It is currently undertaking to establish a monograph procurement instrument which will facilitate library acquisitions. A task force of the committee is examining the potential for shared acquisitions. Although the committee is not an instrument for setting standards, it nevertheless has brought about a certain amount of conformity among the libraries who participate in its programs. As individual library budgets become more constrained and advantages of sharing become more apparent, newer and more far-reaching programs will be undertaken by the FLICC. Shared collection development, or cooperative buying, are a way for federal scientific and technical libraries to continue to provide their users access to vast amounts of information, at less cost to already diminishing budgets.

A number of information policy issues are developing which will have major, and unfavorable, impacts on all federal libraries. The addition of a "sensitive" classification to information which is unclassified, primarily technical, would undoubtedly limit the accessibility of this information to the U.S. researchers served by the federal libraries, as well as to foreign nationals and others perceived to have ulterior motives in their use of this information. The Defense Department's proposed restriction on foreign access to certain U.S. databases, again primarily scientific and technical ones, would eventually restrict the information which organizations are willing to include in these databases, thus preventing the users of the federal libraries from gaining access to important information, including their own and that of other government agencies.

More far reaching than these policy concerns is the currently developing policy which states that ownership of information created under government contracts belongs to the contractor, and not the government. In essence, this means that federal libraries will be forced to buy back more and more of their own agency's data and that of other government agencies. Much government information may never be issued, should the contractor find it too costly to make it available.

The move toward consolidation and coordination of agency information activities continued through the 1970s, although events were most visible in the early years of the decade. The consolidation of agencies collecting weather data, oceanographic information, and information on marine life resulted in the formation of NOAA. The AEC became the Energy Research and Development Agency (ERDA), then the Federal Energy Administration (FEA), and culminated in the Department of Energy, consolidating agency functions and merging areas of responsibility throughout each regrouping. Besides the administrative consolidations, there was a renewed pattern of technological sharing among these scientific and technical agencies. Such examples include NASA's RECON system used by the AEC the three national libraries joining together to create a periodicals data program and agencies learning from each other how to develop and use bibliographic and numeric databases. Libraries often negotiated jointly for operational support through FLICC's FEDLINK.

Computers enabled many types of information centers to burgeon, both as information sources and as distribution points for multi-office or agency materials. The opportunities for resource sharing, broad distribution of publications or data, and the production of information in an array of formats were major achievements brought about by increasingly efficient automation systems and the increased proficiencies of developers and operators. Communications technology also resulted in innovations in information transfer between longer and longer distances, and in more rapid time. The development of networks, such as the one at the NLM, spread the access and receipt of information/data to a broader geographic area in the U. S., and eventually worldwide. The NLM shines like a star in its achievements in developing MEDLARS, MEDLINE, and now GRATEFUL MED, and in bringing them to more recipients in a progressively more user friendly way. NAL has produced its *Park Industries Handbook* on CD-ROM. There is no reason to believe that these developments and the spread of networks will cease, since technological advancements are bringing reduced costs to hardware and software, and the advantages inherent in the application of technology to information handling and transfer have long been proven.

The development of standards for the technology and records needed to control scientific data were made the responsibility of the NBS. NBS established federal standards for information processing, and provided assistance in the development of voluntary ADP standards. For many years, the advantages of COSATI over MARC for scientific and technical information has been argued. With the evolution of national systems and networks, the development of standards for all levels of information processing have continued to be a central aspect of agency discussion and cooperation.

From the literature published about the 1970s and 1980s, the most active agencies moving toward networks were the National Library of Medicine, the National Agricultural Library, the Library of Congress, the National Aeronautics and Space Administration, and the Defense Technical Information Center (DTIC). Some of the other military projects and programs were equally productive but most of their achievements are not discussed in the general literature. The libraries and information centers named above have been working on on-line interactive systems accessible via terminals from remote locations. As telecommunications and satellite transmissions have progressed, so have the systems and their networks. The 1980s have witnessed succeeding attempts to use computers and so related peripheral equipment to design engineering plans/equipment models, to publish final publications, to create and transmit textual and graphic information, and to electronically produce, store, and disseminate a variety of types of data. Improvements and more sophisticated uses will probably be the mainstay of the next several years, with the primary new focus on more direct user contact and less third-party intervention. This will almost certainly impact the way federal libraries go about their business.

Besides concerns with hardware, software, and telecommunications, the late 1970s and 1980s saw a shift in the federal librarian's concerns over his/her professional standing, benefits, and future opportunity. The reexamination of the GS ratings and qualifications by the OPM went on for several years. Likewise, the new pressures of OMB's A-76 on contracting out of noninherently governmental services to commercial firms have created uncertainty and havoc among librarians in the Civil Service. They now fear not only for the dignity and quality of their profession and successors in federal libraries and information centers, but also for their own positions and careers. Ironically, many of the required management studies and management decisions would have been wise courses had it been under the cloud of having their libraries/centers and positions hanging in the balance. There is a growing sense that the A-76 program is not working as had been anticipated and numerous new ideas for ways to reduce the cost of government are surfacing. Federal libraries find a decreased interest in A-76 over the coming years, but economic constraints will not decrease the pressures which will be applied on all governmental entities to operate efficiently and reduce expenditures.

Scientific and technical libraries in the federal sector will realign their programs and services to more appropriately meet the needs of their users in the future. This will mean some major adjustments in the way services are provided, and it will certainly increase the use of technology to support operations, products, and services. Specialized libraries will remain integral, and vital, instruments of those agencies carrying out essential research and technical programs for the benefit of the nation.

REFERENCES

1. Adkinson, Burton W.; *Two centuries of federal information*. Stroudsberg, Pa: Dowden, Hutchinson and Ross; c1978.
2. Evans, Luther H.; *Federal departmental libraries: a summary report of a survey and a conference*. Washington, D.C.: Department of Health, Education and Welfare; 1968.
3. Kent, Allen et al.; *Encyclopedia of library and information science*. New York: Marcel Dekker; 1968-1986.
4. National Center for Education Statistics and the Federal Library Committee; *Survey of federal libraries, Fiscal year 1972*. Washington, D.C.: Department of Health, Education and Welfare; 1975.
5. Stone, Elizabeth W.; *American library development*. New York: H.W. Wilson Co.; 1977.

Corporate Science and Technology Libraries: One Hundred Years of Progress

Edythe Moore

SUMMARY. This paper traces the growth and development of corporate libraries from their nineteenth century beginnings to the present date; notes the major factors which have influenced their development; and relates many of the innovative changes in systems, procedures, and services in these libraries to the ingenuity and dedication of corporate librarians.

In 1987 when we look at the numbers, size, complexity, and sophistication of corporate libraries which exist today, and when we consider the range of services they provide, our first inclination may be to express wonderment that very few, if any, formal corporate libraries existed at all one hundred years ago. However, we need only to consider the phenomenal changes which have taken place in the world-at-large during this same period of time to understand the rapid development of libraries, especially scientific and technical libraries, in the corporate world.

Three major factors influenced their early development; the expansion of research and scholarly publishing, the rapid acceleration in the growth of business and industry, and the newly emerging library profession.[1] Later influences included the tremendous advancements in technology brought about by two world wars, the

---

Edythe Moore is Manager, Charles C. Lauritsen Library, The Aerospace Corporation, Los Angeles, CA 90009. She has a BS in physics from Pennsylvania State University and the MLS from the University of Southern California. She is a past president of the Special Libraries Association and was named a Fellow by the organization in 1987.

U.S. Government's sponsorship of research and development, and the large-scale government endeavors such as space exploration.

EARLY DEVELOPMENT: PRE-WORLD WAR I

Many historians have felt that the mercantile and mechanics libraries, so prevalent in the 1830s and 1840s, were forerunners of the corporate library. Others have credited the establishment by urban public libraries of library deposit and delivery stations in businesses and manufacturing firms with influencing the formation of company libraries. However, Anthony Kruzas[2] in his comprehensive research on the development of business and industrial libraries from 1820-1940, noted that the objectives of the deposit and delivery stations were more closely allied to those of public libraries, i.e., "the betterment of individuals through reading and study." He found that no direct causal relationship existed between either the mercantile and mechanical libraries or the public library deposit and delivery stations and the formation of company libraries. Corporate libraries came into being primarily to further the work of the corporate entity and only secondarily for the improvement of the individual employee.

Kruzas concluded that the true antecedents of company libraries were the working collections of informational materials acquired for business and industrial firms without a conscious intent to establish a library. Indeed, his conclusion is reinforced by the fact that this evolutionary process, especially in small and newly formed companies, has continued well into the twentieth century.

From the earliest days of business and industry, a body of literature, no matter how small, existed to support the work of the company. This literature, the working tools of individual employees or departments within the organization, took many forms. In addition to standard reference treatises and professional scientific and technical periodicals of specific interest to the firm's business, these collections often contained materials such as clippings, pamphlets, and patent files, maps and statistical compilations, and specifications and standards—whatever data the professional employees of the company needed to do their daily work.

Eventually these scattered collections might be brought together and housed in one location. Then what commonly happened was that one or more of the individuals who regularly used these materials became expert in pinpointing specific data within the various resources for both themselves and others. As the collection grew, one of these experts either assumed, or was given, the full-time responsibility for alerting others on the technical staff of new advancements and for excerpting and/or abstracting technical articles, reports, patents, and the like. As often as not, this subject specialist also happened to be a "born librarian and organizer."[3]

In these early days, then, there were apt to be employees with the working title, even if only informal, or botanist/librarian, physician/librarian, engineer/librarian, or chemist/librarian, the latter commonly referred to as a literature chemist. The field of chemistry was one of the first of the scientific disciplines to recognize that the art and science of research in the literature of the field was an important corollary to research at the laboratory bench, and that training in both areas was essential in the education of future chemicals. In later years many literature chemists were hired to head libraries in fields other than chemistry, for the simple reasons that they had training in one of the scientific disciplines and were experienced in the use of the technical literature.

The Kruzas documentation shows that during the last half of the nineteenth century, following the Civil War, there were in existence as many as a dozen chemical, pharmaceutical, consulting, and engineering firms which established "libraries," the size and scope of which were dependent upon the activities of the companies involved. In the early 1900s, two enlightened and progressive librarians—George W. Lee at Stone and Webster and Guy E. Marion at Arthur D. Little, Inc.—established the basic concepts of modern-day company libraries. They recognized early on that the corporate library's basic commodity is information whose value is measured in terms of currency, specificity, and applicability to corporate requirements.

Both Lee and Marion stressed the efficiency and general effectiveness of a centralized information unit whose resources and services would enhance the firm's competitive position. They set out to collect resources which had not been systematically controlled and indexed by the traditional library community, but which were important to their organizations' conduct of business-resources such as internally generated progress reports and analyses of their firm's past research. Recognizing the importance of speed and timeliness in disseminating published information, they instituted current awareness and alerting services such as weekly bulletins of library accessions. They abstracted and indexed journal articles in pertinent company or departmental fields-of-interest. They kept track of unpublished and to-be-published resources. Most significantly, they emphasized the value of providing complete information service — the answering of on-the-spot reference questions and the packaging of data compliations for information research needs.

Both men are credited with changing the form of their respective libraries from a conventional professional collection to a more dynamic company centered information department which they called the corporate information bureau or information center. Throughout corporate library history, many corporate librarians, agreeing that "information center" more accurately reflects the mission and services of their organizations, renamed their library the Technical Information Center (TIC) — a trend which became increasingly popular in the years following World War II.

Lee and Marion, and others of their time, initiated many systems and services that have become hallmarks of the corporate library. The most dynamic of these can be considered to be the corporate library's philosophy of reference/information service.

WORLD WAR I—1940

Industries proliferated in the early 1920s after the first world war and those that already existed grew quickly in size. The number of corporate libraries also multiplied. The libraries were now recognized as a decided corporate asset or, as one prominent librarian of that period noted, industry "has become aware that experience crystallized in print is a tool which may be used as effectively as any part of its accumulated capital."[4]

Corporate librarians were enthusiastic about their new responsibilities for supplying information which would further the work of their companies. But there were problems, too. Or perhaps the practitioners of that day would have preferred to call them challenges. There were no standard practices for acquiring and processing many of the resources not commonly handled by the larger library community. Traditional classification and indexing schemes were too broad to be used for small specialized collections. And interlibrary loan procedures were too cumbersome, the responses to requests too slow.

These librarians, without hesitation, turned to their colleagues who had the same or similar problems; to the Special Libraries Association (SLA) which had been formed in 1909 and which was beginning to be organized into both geographically designated chapters and subject-oriented divisions; and to the technical professional societies that produced publications pertinent to the work of their respective companies.

Working together they developed classification and subject heading schemes for small collections in a particular subject field and pooled them at the SLA headquarters office so they could be made available to others. They met together to share information about new suppliers they had found; new resources, both published and unpublished, which had come to their attention; and new services they had instituted in their own libraries. They took judicious shortcuts in traditional library practices and streamlined procedures. They compiled local area directories of corporate libraries, which pinpointed collection subject strengths, and union lists of serials/ journals.

One of the most interesting happenings in the corporate library world of the 1920s and 1930s was the tremendous amount of "voluntary" work accomplished. These dedicated librarians, willingly and with great spirit, devoted many hours of their own time to assembling the necessary data for publishing the directories and union lists in order that they might give more efficient and effective service to their organizations.

It was a period of demonstrated close-knit unity where both individual and shared responsibilities were highlighted. It was networking at its best—many decades before the concept of networking began to be talked about by more tradition-oriented librarians. And with networking, another hallmark of corporate libraries came into being.

Corporate library development during the years between the two world wars is often cited as an outstanding feature of general library history. There is no doubt but that it was the enthusiastic and dedicated pioneering efforts of the practitioners of the time that produced a vitality which stimulated that development.

POST-WORLD WAR II

Just as had happened after WWI, there was a tremendous growth in the numbers of corporate libraries, especially in scientific and technical areas, immediately following WWII. Established companies endeavored to catch up after giving their time and attention to the war effort, and new companies sprang into existence to take advantage of a whole array of sophisticated technologies developed for the military and which they now planned to use to provide products and services for civilian use.

Not only did corporate libraries proliferate following the war, but they also rapidly expanded in size of collections, staff, and services offered. Burgeoning research and development, much of it sponsored by the U.S. Government, flooded the technical community with a growing body of literature more interdisciplinary in nature than ever before and in new formats. The technical report became popular as a means of rapid and informal communication and took its place alongside the journal literature as the most current and therefore the most important forms of material in the corporate library collection. In many libraries in the industrial sector, technical reports far outnumber all other forms of publications combined.

Getting technical reports under bibliographic control proved to be a major undertaking because of the large number of access points required for retrieval. Their content analysis was a problem because available standard subject heading lists were not designed to handle the specificity required in indexing them. Small libraries utilized semi-automated document handling systems such as Termatrex and Uniterm, but these systems became unwieldy and inefficient to use when the collection reached a certain size. Others, faced with the onslaught of technical report literature, used their firms' computers to prepare Permuted Title Indexes, Keyword in Context (KWIC), and Keyword out of Context (KWOC), as quick-and-dirty, temporary systems until such time as they could devise more suitable ones.

Many corporate libraries undertook large-scale lexicographic projects to build their own thesauri for use in indexing the report literature. Later, when online systems became prevalent, these thesauri also provided the indexing vocabulary for other forms of literature, including the monograph.

In the early 1960s various government bodies joined forces with the Engineers Joint Council (EJC), in Project LEX, for the purpose of constructing a thesaurus of terms applicable to the scientific and technical literature, both discipline-oriented and mission-oriented. Subject specialists from corporate libraries, working in newly developing fields such as the aerospace sciences with its rapidly changing and fluid terminology, were invited to Washington to serve on special task forces for the purpose of hammering out and agreeing on the most appropriate and most up-to-the-minute vocabularies. The libraries that participated in these endeavors carried on the corporate library tradition of cooperation, knowing full well that the rewards, both for them and for the library community in general, would be far greater than their own contribution.

Corporate libraries continued to innovate. They followed the use of Keysort systems for building special subject files and for circulation control, with punched card systems and batch computer operations in the preparation of book catalogs. In the mid-1960s and early 1970s, several corporate libraries pioneered in developing online integrated systems which handled all of their routine recordkeeping tasks, as well as providing subject retrieval. Online capability made corporate networks possible.

When commercially developed online bibliographic databases came on the market in the 1970s, technical libraries put them to immediate use. For the smaller libraries, database searching provided important value-added services. For the larger ones, it meant that they could provide customized information research on a more timely basis.

The advent of numeric databases, electronic document delivery, and full text electronic retrieval enabled the libraries to substitute cost effectively "pay-as-you-go" for purchase and ownership of the most infrequently used reference materials.

Over the years, individual company libraries have had various corporate responsibilities for materials other than formally published externally and internally generated publications. Guy Marion in 1910 was successful in having the correspondence of the various departments routed through his library so that the information could be indexed.[2] Later smaller corporate libraries frequently were given complete control of correspondence and other company informational materials such as laboratory notebooks. It was not uncommon for libraries in smaller companies to handle the corporate-wide control of security classified materials. As corporations became larger these functions also grew and became separate corporate units. In the 1980s, however, there is a trend back toward the corporate libraries, especially the larger ones, assuming the responsibility for company information-related functions such as records management programs, corporate archival systems, the control of microcomputer software, the primary and the secondary distribution of internally-generated reported, and the corporate classified document control systems.

This trend makes good sense. Parent organizations recognize the library's demonstrated expertise in the systematic organization and control of large quantities of materials in a wide variety of formats. And corporate libraries, operating in an integrated information environment, are able to provide "one stop" information service for the company's employees.

1988 AND BEYOND

When John Naisbitt[5] in 1982 suggested that our society "is living in the time of the parenthesis" — in a time between eras — corporate librarians may have felt that his descriptive phrase also characterizes the transitional stages in corporate library development: one foot in the past, but stepping into the future; professionally tied to traditional librarianship, but propelled forward by time and place to innovations in systems and services; always with corporate librarians committed to logical and necessary transitions along the development continuum.

There is little cause to believe that corporate libraries will proceed any differently through the information age — either while still inside, or on the far side of the parenthesis—unless it is at an even faster pace. A corporate information unit will continue to have a vital role in any industrial or research organization if company employees are to receive the information they need to do their work. This information unit probably will not be called a library, but its mission and basic functions will remain the same as the information centers of Lee and Marion. What most surely will be changed will be the architecture. Regardless of the unit's name, the word *system* will describe more adequately the "library's" new structure: the corporate information system.

At some point in the near term, it is likely that the once-called library will have become a switching center for a decentralized operation in a fully integrated corporate information environment. The need for increased degrees of cooperation between the unit's functional groups, already well developed in industrial libraries, will give rise to matrix organizational schemes rather than hierarchical lines of authority and decision-making.

The array and variety of services offered will be different. New service lines or user groupings are entirely possible. One scenario may find some of the information professionals physically located with a working group, although it is likely that in the future there may be less departmentalization within the corporate environment. Some individuals believe that the information age will bring about a "decline in the professions," that one of their special strengths, acting as exclusive repositories and disseminators of their special knowledge, may be considerably diminished.[6] The same might be said for other speciality technical groups within the corporation.

Members of the staff of the corporate information system will continue to be expert in the field of literature at a time when scientific and technical information will no longer be thought of as different in kind or quantity from that which is economic, managerial, or personal. Sophisticated indexing systems will have closed the gap. In addition, tomorrow's information professionals may be expected to serve also as architect, guide, consultant, trainer, catalyst, or synergist in the integrated information environment. In any case, members of the staff of the information unit will move closer to the day-to-day work and to the product of the organization.

It has been suggested that technology develops in three phases.

First, it enables us to do what we can do now, only cheaper, faster, and better. Second, it enables us to do what we cannot do now. Third, it changes our life-styles.[7] For the many reasons previously cited, including but not limited to technological advances, we can think of these phases as being comparable to phases along the corporate library's development continuum. Currently performing many services that it could not have accomplished just a few years ago, the corporate library is laying the groundwork for entry into the third phase. Preparations are underway for a new "life-style" — a new structure and new methods of operation. Its mission, however, will remain the same. Information has been the industrial library's major resource since the days of Lee and Marion. Information service has always been its *raison d'être*. These factors will not change.

REFERENCES

1. Christianson, Elin B. Special Libraries: Putting knowledge to work. *Library Trends*. 25(1): 399-416; 1976 July.
2. Kruzas, Anthony T. *Business and industrial libraries in the United States: 1820-1940*. New York: Special Libraries Association; 1965.
3. Joannes, Edith. A fifty-year old technical library. *Special Libraries*. 30: 254-7; 1939 October.
4. Rankin, Rebecca B. Reminiscences of the first fifty years by former presidents of SLA. *Stechert-Hafner Book News*. 13: 79-82; 1959 March.
5. Naisbitt, John. *Megatrends: Ten new directions transforming our lives*. New York: Warner; 1982.
6. Evans, Christopher. *The mighty micro*. London: Gollancz; 1979.
7. Featheringham, T. R. Paperless publishing and potential institutional change. *Scholarly Publishing*. 13(1): 19-30; 1981 October.

Information-Retrieval:
A 35-Year Personal Perspective

Everett H. Brenner

SUMMARY. Presented as the "Miles Conrad Memorial Lecture" at the 29th Annual Conference of the National Federation of Abstracting and Information Services" on March 1, 1987. The author presents a personal view of the rise of computer operations in information retrieval as seen by an indexing manager over his career.

In a recent *New York Times* article entitled "Learning on the Job," A. M. Rosenthal, Associate Editor of the *Times*, wondered whether in 40 years as a newspaperman he had learned "one damned thing." "'I've decided," he wrote, "that yes, I have indeed learned a few things. Some had to do with newspapering, some with the world; a couple were about flowers, a few about the *Times* and one or two about myself. All told, eight or nine things or roughly one every five years, which is not too bad when you think about it."

These seem to be my sentiments after more than 35 years in information work, and I would like to share with you a few incidents and influences from my experience. As we proceed you may feel that the events I expand upon are rather simple, even mundane, but I hope you will see that the implications have, over time, affected a great many important decisions. And, in fact, good decisions for future progress are only made by understanding a problem on its simplest level and in perspective (a favorite word of mine, as many of you know).

These mundane experiences will lead to a discussion on:

Everett H. Brenner is Manager, Central Abstracting & Indexing Service, American Petroleum Institute, 156 William St., New York, NY.

© 1988 by The Haworth Press, Inc. All rights reserved.

I. Accountability and Responsibility
II. An Approach to the Computer World
III. A National Plan for Abstracting and Indexing Services?
IV. Information Environments

I. ACCOUNTABILITY AND RESPONSIBILITY

Thirty years ago I was in charge of an information system in which a major resource was a classified set of abstract cards. One day I discovered a file cabinet containing cards, representing 6 or 8 months of updates, which had never been interfiled. At the same time searchers were using the file, assuming it was complete and up to date, totally unaware that they were missing necessary information. That situation showed me how easy it was to get away with having an unsatisfactory file. Rarely were users able to evaluate the completeness of a file, let alone the accuracy of an indexing or classification system.

The file cabinet and manual card file of yesteryear were far more visible than the computers and computer tapes of today. Neither database producers nor online vendors are held accountable for the quality of today's databases. Most, if not all, databases are missing records, and have incomplete or incorrect data. But it appears that none is the wiser among the users, and corrective action by the suppliers is rare.

At API we had always been especially quality conscious. We recorded mistakes and omissions in our online databases as soon as we became aware of them, with the intention of making corrections as soon as possible. Nevertheless, our first efforts to implement a correction process took 9 years. That is, it was 9 years from when we asked the online vendor to provide correction capability to when we did our first correction run. Even then the correction process was so cumbersome that one did not want to use it very often. Lately, I'm glad to say, things have improved. We now have straightforward methods of correcting errors in our databases. But I do understand that there are still vendors that have no mechanism whatsoever for correcting errors.

Just as yesterday's users never reacted to incomplete card files neither do today's online searchers complain much about shoddy databases. Even the professional intermediary maintains silence. But today's searchers are more fortunate than their predecessors; they have ready access to multiple databases, thanks to online systems, so that the failings of one file may be offset by another, when similar files exist. This eases the problem of faulty databases, but it causes high searching costs which we seem to accept without questioning. The database producer is thus lulled into inaction.

For the future, a word of caution. In this age of the aggressive lawyer, the future may hold problems for bibliographic database producers and vendors who flagrantly ignore responsibility for database quality. At last year's EUSIDIC meeting. Peter Seipel of Sweden presented a truly ominous paper entitled "Do you Guarantee Your Data? A View of Liability" in which he described, hypothetically, what could happen when an information consumer uses incorrect information and holds the provider responsible. Those missing cards of 30 years ago that I spoke of could come back to haunt us.

II. AN APPROACH TO THE COMPUTER WORLD

Now I want to report two of my early computer-related experiences.

The first event took place in the 1950s. While working on a keyword list for an index, I used a card sorter to get a few hundred keypunched cards into approximate alphabetical order, by sorting on the first three characters. For those of you too young or too sophisticated who may not be familiar with a card sorter, let me say that each character sorted required a pass of all the cards through the machine. Thus if I wanted to alphabetize on the first 15 characters, I would have to make 15 passes, taking five times as long as for three characters. Since my cards had as many as 20 characters of data, a complete sort would have required 20 passes; thus sorting on only three characters was a time saver. It then struck me that I really could control the effort of the machine much more closely than that of a human being. It is most difficult for a human being to sort "approximately." Had I tried to sort the cards manually in approximate order, I would have spent nearly as much time as for getting them in absolute order. This was a case of the machine having a kind of flexibility that a human being lacks. Thus to take full advantage of a computer is not simply to duplicate the human, but rather to improve on the human and make feasible otherwise unrealistic tasks.

For example, making concordances is not a job for human beings. It is true that concordances of the Bible have been prepared by monks working in monasteries. But these have been dedicated men, devoting their lives to one project, sacrificing any possible normal human life. In fact, one of my students doing a paper on biblical concordances found a reference that reported a high incidence of madness in monks who worked on Bible concordances.

Can we imagine a monk producing his concordance? He starts working his way through the text of the Bible, making an index card for each word, the card recording the word and the verse in which it occurred. As long as he has no more than 20 or 30 cards, if he encounters a second occurrence of the word, he remembers, picks up the card, and makes another verse entry. Soon, however, the pack of cards gets too big for his memory. So he alphabetizes the cards. Now for each word of the text he looks through his deck to see if there is a card for this word. If the card exists, he removes it from the deck, makes another verse entry, and refiles the card. If the word is new, he makes a new card and interfiles it alphabetically. But what about possible mistakes? To be safe, at the end of his work day, he reviews all of the work that he has done. And despite his review, errors creep in. The procedure is indeed maddening.

Now, how does a computer make a concordance? Perhaps, this way. Using a magnetic tape containing the full text of the Bible, it scans the tape word by word, making a separate record of word and verse number for each word. When it has gone through the entire tape, it has one record for each word in the Bible. Next it sorts all these records in alphabetical order by word. Then it scans the sorted list, eliminating the duplicate words and making a single record for each unique word with all the verse numbers in which it is found. The result is the concordance.

Look at all the extra work the computer has done. First, it has made the equivalent of an index card, not for each unique word, but for every occurrence of every word. Second, it has gone through the process of sorting this gigantic stack of records. But all of this is effortless.

So you see, concordance making is a job for the computer, not for humans. The prime modern-day kind of concordance, made possible by computers, is Eugene Garfield's "Science Citation Index," of course.

If we take the traditional classification system or a subject index and make it machine readable and searchable, there is not much advantage and the computer has done little. A computerized card catalog saves floor space, but otherwise is little improvement over an old-fashioned card catalog. Briefly, it is not enough for the computer to duplicate a simple human effort; being machine readable is not enough. But look at the additional capabilities the computers can give us. We can set up a system using controlled or uncontrolled keywords and abstracts, and search it by complex Boolean expressions with links, proximity, and other helping devices. The computer makes other approaches to searching feasible, such as full-text searching, a job that would be unthinkable by human effort alone. Term association, probabilities, and syntactical enhancements can make searching by computer even more effective. Further in the future are expert systems and other approaches to artificial intelligence. These will make it possible for us to process information and search on a quality level not dreamed of in the past.

The second incident took place in the early 1960s when we at API were designing our computerized information retrieval system. It was a meeting of information staff with a group of computer experts from various oil companies. We information people kept describing processes we wanted to run on the machine. For whatever we asked, the computer people said "Yes. We can do that." There was nothing the machine couldn't do. But, there was a big "but." We had to be willing to pay for the effort to make the machine do it. The limit on the machine's ability was not creativity but money.

This led me to formulate an approach to system design. The computer allows me to consider systems to satisfy my wildest dreams and ideals. I will be limited only by my own creative abilities and imagination. After I design this seemingly wild but feasible system I am aware that I have to compromise because computer costs will limit me. By designing in modular fashion, I can remove features until I have a more limited system that is inside my economic constraints. But the unused modules are available, ready to be added to the system whenever economic conditions or improvements in computing permit.

A great advantage to this approach to computer system design is that the information manager is more in control of the computer and the computer expert. Instead of scouting out new computer capabilities and asking computer people what's available, the information manager tells the computer expert what he wants to do, makes clear that he knows the computer capability is there, and simply asks of the computer expert that he outline the ease and cost of implementation. Good computer people will appreciate and respect that you are in charge of the specifications of the system.

My experience with the card sorter led me to marvel at the potential of the computer and technology in general. My meeting with computer people clued me in to how best to use the potential.

III. A NATIONAL PLAN FOR ABSTRACTING AND INDEXING SERVICES?

In April 1962, NFAIS (then called NFSAIS) employed Robert Heller and Associates to develop "a national plan and program defining the present and future role of science abstracting, indexing, and reviewing services of the United States." The results of the Heller group's work were presented to the NFSAIS annual conference 24 years ago, in March 1963. The advent and understanding of the Heller Report was important to me in defining the API services and their place in the information arena.

Heller described two categories of databases; profession-oriented and project-oriented. The profession-oriented type covers everything in a particular branch of knowledge, such as chemistry, physics, or sociology. This is a pure knowledge approach, far removed from the needs of business and industrial users. To serve the latter, there was the project-oriented database. This was interdisciplinary, taking from various fields of knowledge the information needed by the more specialized industrial and government researcher. Project-oriented databases are much closer to the user; they are flexible and responsive to changing information needs. The Heller report recommended formation of an "Organization X" to administer a brokering operation to gather products from the profession-oriented services based on the requests of the project-oriented services. The requests would be based on current needs of the end users. There would be no reabstracting or reindexing.

What would result? Well, if Organization X were set up, the profession-oriented organization would have a source of income from Organization X; Organization X would be funded by the project-oriented organizations; and the users would get faster, better service, at lower cost. But to do this successfully required some drastic steps. First of all, the profession-oriented databases would need adequate funding to be fully comprehensive. They would also have to be organized to do quick, accurate finding, abstracting, and indexing. They would have to deliver finished abstracts in a convenient and more standardized form for use by the project-oriented groups. In turn, the project-oriented information services would have to be willing to give up turf. They would have to agree to stop their own journal scanning, abstracting, etc., and to set themselves up to cull what they needed from the profession-oriented groups and repackage it. But this was not a plan for abolishing any data bases. Miles Conrad noted in 1963 that the Heller staff "have recognized the great importance of the continued autonomy of the members of the Federation [NFSAIS] and yet . . . have been able to suggest means by which the work of the Federation can be enhanced and expanded and at the same time provide for us a mechanism that can assure not merely cooperation but true and effective coordination of our efforts."

And what was the result of that grand plan? Not much. Chemical Abstracts and Biological Abstracts have since instituted cooperative activities that avoid some duplication. API's patent abstracts service consists more than 90% of repackaged Derwent abstracts. But apart from these groups and one or two others, nothing has happened. The profession-oriented groups have largely not been strengthened. The project-oriented services are not repackaging to any significant extent. They maintain their independent abstracting and indexing systems. Standards exist but standardization of abstracts or indexes between services is practically nonexistent. The searcher has no certainty about the coverage of any of the databases. Most profession-oriented databases cannot be trusted to be absolutely comprehensive. So searchers doing exhaustive searches must use several databases to be sure that the field of interest is really covered. Project-oriented databases seldom begin to meet the whole needs of an industrial user. As a result, many users have taken to downloading portions of multiple databases and constructing their own private interdisciplinary databases.

Although the recommendations of the Heller Report were never implemented, the Report's description of the services as profession-oriented or project-oriented and its analysis of the economic problems facing the services is as valid in the database time-shared online world of today as it was in the printed abstract and index world of that time. Today, without Organization X, databases of all kinds are put into the online pot and all the producers, profession-oriented as well as project-oriented, market extensively to the users. Thus the not-for-profits, mostly disciplinary file organizations, are as aggressive and competitive as the for-profits, who are most often selling the interdisciplinary, project-oriented files. The database vendors are also aggressively marketing all their products, these same databases. The users are mostly confused by all these available riches, and only wise and experienced intermediaries are able to cleverly sort out and plan a strategy to use multiple databases effectively.

Why was Organization X never implemented? In retrospect I believe it's because it was an un-American approach. A free and open society such as ours doesn't readily submit to National Plans. I often wonder where our university people, who are always consulting on national plans in Third World Countries, get their experience—certainly not here in the U.S. Organization X required too many restrictions on too many independent services, at least in the process of initiating the implementation.

However, since its real value was in its definition of bibliographic services and analysis of their use, there is still value we can derive from the Report, though not on a national plan level. A database can review its kindred databases and analyze the kind of file it is selling and how close it is to the pulse of the user. Such a review may discover great economic savings and efficiencies by repackaging and by cooperative efforts. Many industrial information centers have been cutting back on research and information use. This means reduced income to the database industry. Therefore database producers will need new ideas to even maintain effectiveness. Perhaps rereading the Heller Report can lead to ideas to help reduce costs without compromising the quality and comprehensiveness of the products.

IV. INFORMATION ENVIRONMENTS

I have managed API's information and database services since 1959. From 1965 to 1979 I also taught information science courses in a library school. When friends asked me what I did for a living, they were not particularly enlightened when I told them that I managed an abstracting and indexing service and built databases for the petroleum industry. They were even more confused when I said I also taught in a library school although I had never earned a library school degree nor even taken a library course. But it's not at all remarkable. As a post-World War II information scientist in an industrial environment, I was one of many in the midst of a whole new world of information processing.

The information departments were being run by nonlibrarians, using the library as only one of an array of resources. The air was thick with descriptors, keywords, concept coordination, thesaurus and other new information elements. These were supplementing, indeed superseding, the traditional library indexes and classification systems. But to use these new tools effectively, it was necessary to understand how they came into being, what their relationship was to the tools that they were largely replacing. For example, keywords were becoming a major indexing tool. If one was to really understand what a keyword was, one would have to understand how it differed from the traditional subject heading, the province of the librarian.

Over the last 30 years, much progress has been made by the information scientists and even more by the librarians. It is important to note the subtle similarities and the subtle differences in their approaches. So is it also important to understand the differences between the industrial center environment where for the most part the nonlibrary-educated "information scientist" has reigned and the academic and public library environments, where the library-educated "information scientist" has operated.

Let us analyze these environments historically in terms of online searching. In each of the settings—the public library, the university library and the industrial information center—the need for an intermediary in searching online databases became evident very early. This need held true even in environments where traditionally no intermediary was provided for searching by manual tools. When automated search systems were introduced, the end user and the information specialist encountered difficulties that had not been encountered in the manual tools environment.

Let's look first at the public library user. Historically, the public library provided services which simply pointed the user to the appropriate tools and left him to his own devices to ferret out the information. Frequently, the public library end user is seeking a quick reference, a few selected bibliographic references. Such a result is obtainable by searching through printed indexes and the library's catalog. It is rare that the end user in this environment requires an extensive, in-depth search of the literature. Therefore, he has traditionally met his or her own needs with very little intervention on the part of an intermediary. Where online searching has been offered to the public library user, the traditional approach changed radically. The user no longer sought and retrieved his or her own information. An intermediary and a fee were imposed between the user and the information.

The university library has also traditionally been an end user environment where the student and professor did their own searching. It was their job to go to the library and search literature, read what they had uncovered, and search again. Their business of learning and teaching forced them to delve into the reference material. Thus, information retrieval was an integral part of the definition of their roles as teachers and students. When online searching was introduced, the end user environment changed dramatically to an intermediary environment, an anomaly for a university setting. End users were not permitted to use online search facilities for fear they would be misused and become an economic hazard. Visions of users spending hundreds of hours combining terms and printing references could simply not be permitted to become a reality.

Now however this very same public library/university library environment, which had moved from a seemingly successful end user environment to an intermediary environment in which the user was viewed with trepidation and suspicion, is "normalizing"—by returning to the traditional modus operandi, permitting end users to do their own searching. The professionals in this environment want to believe that enhanced proximity searching, truncation, and "lead-in" techniques will significantly simplify end user efforts. They believe that online availability of natural language, full-text files has made searching more conducive to end user participation. However, the fact is that searching natural language requires infinitely more sophistication than searching with structured search terms. The end user's search results will be poorer. Indeed, the university librarians have permitted the entrepreneurs to sell them a bill of goods because their roots lie in the end user philosophy and their desire is to return to what has historically been "normal" for them.

When we look at the information center in an industrial setting, we see a very different environment where the norm is very alien to the two settings we have just analyzed. This environment has always operated with a true intermediary philosophy. Unlike the role of the student or the professor, whose business it is to read and search the literature, it is the role of professionals in industry to do: to carry out applied research, to develop products, to test new markets. They have not been hired to read. However, the importance of literature searching has never been minimized by industry. Therefore, it has traditionally been essential to employ technical staff—an intermediary—to deliver relevant and complete information to professional staff of industrial organizations.

Prior to the advent of online systems, the information staff intermediaries searched the manual indexes thoroughly and understood the interactive nature of bibliographic searching. Their methods treated hard copy indexes in the same way as they would afterwards handle online files. Therefore, the transition to online searching occurred easily and without the apprehension experienced in other environments.

The only noticeable change was quite positive. Turnaround time significantly improved. Exhaustive searches of the literature could be delivered almost immediately. As productivity increased, so did the demand for information services. Therefore, the staff of industrial information centers grew.

But then the late 70s and early 80s brought cutbacks. In order to continue to provide quick, thorough retrieval while reducing staff, industrial libraries started training end users to do their own online searching, thereby reversing the historical pattern. The industrial information center briefly became an end user environment. This was not the "normal" environment and the new trend was short-lived. As in the public library or university setting, the tools did not change—no intelligent search systems were made available to the end user. And the end user who started his new searching responsibilities with pleased enthusiasm soon cried for help. The searching "career" of the average end user ended in less than 2 months. Without artificial intelligence built into the search systems, these end users could not effectively manipulate the subtleties of Boolean searching. Just as the university librarian wanted to return to the historical norm, so did users of information centers in industrial settings.

Environments have not been analyzed well by marketers. The academic world, normally an end user environment, is in trouble and uncomfortable in an intermediary-based technology. The industrial world would like to save money but is uncomfortable in a system inadequately set up for end users. CD-ROM is currently being offered as a reduced cost alternative. In CD-ROM, the environment is ripe for music lovers of the world but they are not retrieving information. They do not have to access music by using Boolean algebra. End user environments are not friendly ones for Boolean algebra. CD-ROM is not the answer. We need breakthroughs if we are not to be at the mercy of all our traditional environments. Artificial intelligence systems are the breakthroughs we need.

I learned by becoming a member of a library school faculty how important it was to understand the historical bases of present information systems. Entrepreneurs must take the time to learn a little more about historical perspective and specific information environments. We information scientists need to expand our thinking to better understand our own environments. CD-ROM producers are trying to find a role for their products in information work. We see quoted so much today that optical media is a technology in search of application, a technology in search of a market. That is to me a discouraging approach and connotes the great gap that exists between technology and the use of that technology. If we work harder to understand our information environments, the market will be searching for the technology as it should be.

V. BRENNER'S LAWS OF INFORMATION SCIENCE

Besides this paper being a 35-year personal perspective, it has also been written in the spirit of the theme of this meeting, "Demystifying the Database Business. What's Really Happening Behind the Hype?" I love mysteries and demystifying is a special pleasure of mine. And as a devil's advocate, I have conjured up some laws of information science which I hope will consider and perhaps even debate in your deliberations on the hype in the database business today.

1. *Brenner's Law of System Design.* Determine the best system before designing the system you can afford.
2. *Brenner's Law for End User Environments.* Never let a bright end user use a system which can be searched more effectively by a poor intermediary.
3. *Brenner's Law for Entrepreneurs.* Understanding the application of new technology is more important than understanding new technology.
4. *Brenner's Law of Future Systems.* Artificial intelligence systems will be friendly systems but only if they are based on present systems that are intelligent.

Education for Sci-Tech Librarianship: Retrospect and Prospect

Linda C. Smith

SUMMARY. This paper reviews the history of formal educational programs in sci-tech librarianship and suggests likely future developments. Educational programs for sci-tech librarianship are linked to developments in both special librarianship and information science. Aspects considered include student qualifications and recruitment, course offerings and curriculum, faculty and other resources, and teaching methods and special programs. Current trends in library education are identified. Future educational programs must be responsive to the development of new roles, new information sources, and the widespread need for scientific literacy.

On the occasion of the centenary of library education in the United States, it is appropriate to consider the historical development of educational programs for what Hanson has termed "science-information work," defined as "the organization and exploitation, by all appropriate means, of all kinds of information and sources of information used in science and technology."[1] Although historically many science information workers have earned degrees in science or engineering and then learned information-related skills on the job, the focus of this paper is formal educational programs for library and information work in science and technology. The related area of education for medical librarianship is not dealt with.

Linda C. Smith is Associate Professor in the Graduate School of Library and Information Science at the University of Illinois at Urbana-Champaign, Urbana, IL 61801. She holds a PhD from Syracuse University, an MS in information and computer science from Georgia Institute of Technology, an MS in library science from the University of Illinois at Urbana-Champaign, and a BS in mathematics and physics from Allegheny College.

© 1988 by The Haworth Press, Inc. All rights reserved.

RETROSPECT

> Library schools during the past sixty years have given little attention to science, in spite of its growing importance.
>
> *Charles Harvey Brown, 1953*[2]

By the early 1900s there were a number of sci-tech libraries of various types: departmental libraries in universities, sci-tech divisions in some of the major public libraries, government agency libraries, industrial libraries, and libraries in institutions such as herbaria, observatories, and museums. A book entitled *Training for Librarianship: Library Work as a Career*, published in 1921, noted both agricultural libraries and technical libraries as special types.[3] The Special Libraries Association was organized in 1909 and its Science-Technology Division was established in 1924. In spite of these developments, formal library education programs tended to be generalist in nature, with an emphasis on preparing students for work in public and academic libraries. At Columbia University its School of Library Service, which was opened in 1887 as the first library school in the United States, had no special course in science until 1936, when it offered a course known as Bibliographic and Reference Service in Science and Technology.[3a] There were occasional pleas for specially designed programs, such as Orton's statement in 1944: "The need for the preparation of science and technology librarians demands that we drop our aloofness from the scientist and technologist and work out a program acceptable first of all to them, for they are going to be the ones to use the service, and secondly to us."[4] Nevertheless, recommendations on education for special librarianship published in 1954 noted that the recommended programs suggested little deviation from standard courses offered in library schools, because it was felt that special library education could and should be based on the curriculum required by library schools.[5] This sentiment was echoed by Bonn in 1959 when he stated that "library schools should prepare students first of all to be *librarians* and then, and only then, prepare them for specialized positions within the overall framework of professional library work."[6] In 1986 Williams and Zachert noted that the situation still has not changed substantially: "curricula for special librarians stand essentially where they were in the 1920s: a core of courses dealing with matters of concern to all libraries plus a component of elective courses relating to only a few of the potential specializations in the total information industry."[7] As Rossiter observed, "around 1960 there comes a great discontinuity in what is written about science libraries and bibliographies. Suddenly the scene shifts outside the library, and the literature is dominated by the broader concepts of 'information' and more optimistically 'communication'."[8] Marking this shift was a report published in 1961 and entitled *Science Information Personnel: The New Profession of Information Combining Science, Librarianship and Foreign Language*.[9] This report described the elements of science information work, listing 12 presently accepted tasks of science information specialists and 5 recent and significant trends in the profession. The 12 accepted tasks included: administering, locating materials, selecting materials, acquiring materials, descriptive cataloging, subject analyzing (including classifying/subject headings and indexing), abstracting and/or annotating, performing reference work, literature searching-bibliography, transmitting and copying, translating, converting into machinable form. The recent and significant trends included: development of information systems, investigating of machine applications, information interpreting, researching with information, and information scouting. The report recommended the establishment of a new graduate school of science information, with a 1-year graduate curriculum leading to an MS in information. The recommended curriculum included courses on information sources (biomedical sciences and medicine, chemistry, physical sciences and mathematics, engineering), science information center administration, acquisition of science information, description and subject analysis of science information, abstracting and annotating science information, graphics and publication, reference work and retrieval of science information, language and science information, science information theory and systems development, science information instrumentation, and theory and practice of information interpretation and research. The report also suggested the possibility of two different types of doctoral programs, one devoted to the study of literature science and one to systems development.

Over the next few years conferences were held at Georgia Institute of Technology and Western Reserve University to explore further possible programs for the education of science information personnel. Participants in the first Georgia Tech conference recommended the development of graduate programs apart from library schools.[10] Although the 1964 conference at Western Reserve was entitled "The Education of Science Information Personnel," it is evident from the proceedings that many of the participants were in fact addressing the broader concept of information science.[11] This trend is even more pronounced in the proceedings of an international conference on Education for Scientific Information Work held in London in 1967.[12] The confusion of terminology — science information/information — science led Isaac Welt in a 1964 editorial to plead with readers to differentiate clearly between the two.[13] As the concern of this paper lies with education for science information work, the evolution of information science over the past 20 years will not be traced. Instead, a number of issues in the design of educational programs for sci-tech librarianship are addressed: student qualifications and recruitment; course offerings and curriculum; faculty and other resources; and teaching methods and special programs.

Student Qualifications and Recruitment

Although there is some dissent in the literature,[14] it is generally assumed that students interested in pursuing a career in sci-tech librarianship should have at least a bachelor's degree in one of the sciences or engineering. Other qualifications frequently noted as desirable include a general education, familiarity with several foreign languages, and knowledge of the history of science. Some writers also note desirable personal attributes, such as Voigt's list of a "high degree of initiative, imagination, ambition, and interest"[15] and Hunt's list of a "high degree of intelligence, intellectual curiosity, and an excellent memory."[16] Over 40 years ago Hunt noted the difficulty of recruiting qualified science librarians because of low salaries, and she argued for the need for publicity to familiarize science students with opportunities in the library field. In fact, there was one segment of the science student population which had been encouraged to consider careers in science librarianship; as Rossiter observed, "much of the vocational guidance literature of the 1930s addressed to women in science (chemistry especially) urged them to become librarians or abstractors."[17]

Given the ample opportunities for placing students in sci-tech positions, it would seem appropriate for library schools to try to recruit students with backgrounds in science and engineering. A few schools have undertaken such recruitment efforts in the past, but with little long-term effect. As Fasick noted, increased emphasis on technology in library schools should make these schools more attractive to students with sci-tech backgrounds, but it has not happened.[18] Statistics reveal that fewer than 10% of the students enrolled in graduate library science programs hold science degrees. Because there are not enough students with science degrees to go around, libraries are forced to consider candidates with other backgrounds, particularly prior experience in a science library.[19]

Course Offerings and Curricula

Over the years there have been a number of surveys documenting the available library school courses related to special librarianship and including notes on courses specific to sci-tech librarianship. In 1959 Bonn reported the results of an international survey describing worldwide facilities available for training in scientific documentation work.[20] In addition to formal educational programs, he described the programs of professional organizations, practical training on the job or in workshops, home study by correspondence, and continuing education. In 1960 Owens reported that schools surveyed had from one to three courses related to sci-tech librarianship, with particular emphasis on sci-tech literature.[21] There were also some specialized bibliography courses on subjects such as biology, chemistry, and engineering. Ripin and Kasman reported on data collected in 1974-75.[22] The content of courses on sci-tech literature included study and use of sources as well as selection, organization, and collection development in science, with strong emphasis on evaluation of sources. In addition there was often an effort to set the literature in context through study of the structure and methodology of science, historical development of the literature, communication patterns among scientists, and user needs. Topics less frequently mentioned included the role of databases in science, abstracting and indexing services, the role of scientific and technical societies and government in scientific research, and the use of audiovisual materials in science. Finally, a survey completed by Mellott in 1980 demonstrated that sci-tech librarianship is not generally offered as a separate type of library course at present.[23] Library school courses are often limited to special libraries/librarianship and sci-tech literature. Some programs include additional courses in sci-tech literature (or the literature of specific scientific and technical subjects). Opportunities for supervised practical experience in sci-tech libraries are also possible in some programs. The reported content of available courses suggests that many demonstrate a concern for the subject and its practitioners as well as the subject literature and its uses. This is responsive to Shera's description of what a librarian specializing in a subject area should know: "the fundamental principles of the subject, the great events in its historical development, the directions in which its research is progressing, the structure of its literature, and the ways in which that literature is, or may be, used."[24]

The offerings of most schools in sci-tech librarianship follow the recommendations laid out by Voigt in 1954, in that training for all of science and engineering is within a single curriculum because a library school cannot deal with many different specialties.[25] The recommended program included a core common to other areas of librarianship: introduction to librarianship, introductory cataloging and classification, bibliography and reference materials, selection and acquisition of materials, and library administration. Recommended electives included advanced reference work, administration of college and university (or public) libraries, advanced cataloging and classification, government documents, and library human relations and personnel psychology. Courses specific to sci-tech librarianship would include scientific and technical reference sources and materials and their use, organization and control of scientific and technical literature, selection of materials for scientific and technical libraries, and administration of scientific and technical libraries. In addition there would be a special research problem or thesis and/or the opportunity to complete an internship in a technical library. As described above, library schools have not developed this many specialized courses for sci-tech librarianship. The exception for a period in the 1960s was Drexel, which had a special program including the following courses: acquiring and organizing science information, science literature searching, abstracting and annotating, information center administration, instrumentation of information sciences, integration of science information systems, methods of research, case studies in computer programming, industrial management, editing and publication for the professions, and reference materials in science and technology.[26] Other library schools did not follow Drexel's lead. A few programs were established outside of library schools, such as that at Georgia Institute of Technology,[27] but they were short-lived, in some cases evolving into educational programs for information science. Although most library school programs do not support specialization in a particular area of science, there are exceptions, such as Indiana University's chemical information specialist program.[28]

A new development, beginning in the 1970s, was the introduction of courses addressing multidisciplinary fields which include substantial science components. In contrast to the more traditional disciplinary-based bibliography courses in subjects such as chemistry, a course in environmental information must draw on several different subject areas related to the solution of environmental problems. Dosa describes one such course introduced at Syracuse in 1972: contents covered genesis of the environmental concern, characteristics of information behavior in a multidisciplinary field, current and potential users of environmental information, information resources, information systems, information processes (identification, acquisition, organization, management, interpretation, and dissemination), and the international exchange of environmental information.[29]

Faculty and Other Resources

None of the surveys reporting on course offerings included information about the faculty responsible for teaching the courses. A number of authors have commented on the difficulty of finding qualified faculty: "Effective teaching in any field of professional study calls for a combination of successful practical experience at a senior level, academic and professional qualifications and teaching ability. Individuals who match this specification are rare in any profession and, in the case of science information work, the overall shortage of practitioners means that the obvious source of supply is itself very limited."[30] When no regular faculty member has the necessary qualifications to teach sci-tech literature or related courses, the library school must rely on practicing librarians as adjunct faculty members. Another aspect of institutional resources which can affect the quality of course offerings is the strength of library resources available to students. A sci-tech literature course is of limited value if the students do not have ready access to the titles discussed.

Teaching Methods and Special Programs

The most commonly offered specialized course deals with sci-tech literature. Bonn suggested that there are two possible approaches to such a course: by individual subject discipline or by distinctive publication form.[31] Students would work from bibliographies based on standard and comprehensive guides to the reference literature or on holdings of the particular library to which they have access. Matarazzo suggested the case method as an alternative form of instruction.[32] His book includes 35 instructional case studies covering science reference questions, sources, collection development, and policy.

To give students an opportunity to work closely with scientists involved in research, various assignments and special programs have been devised. Representative of those reported in the literature are Wilson's use of an assignment in which students compile a bibliography for a scientist or engineer engaged in funded research;[33] the program for science information specialists at the University of Illinois in which selected students were assigned to special topics advisors, senior members of the science faculty who were actively involved in research and for whom they prepared abstracts, bibliographies and reviews of the literature in a real life setting;[34] and Martin's postgraduate program in which trainees who had completed their master's in library science were assigned to the laboratories of senior scientists and became integral members of working research teams, functioning as information specialists.[35] In each case the intent was to give the student or trainee an opportunity to develop a close working relationship with a scientist. The more ambitious programs depended on outside funding and lasted only a few years; in contrast, assignments of the type suggested by Wilson could be given on a regular basis.

CURRENT TRENDS

The preceding discussion has reviewed issues which have been addressed in the literature on education for sci-tech librarianship over the past 100 years. To mark the centenary of library education, a number of papers have already appeared, giving historical reviews and discussions of current and future trends. Hayes noted as trends the integration of automation, greater demands for admission, greater specialization, greater length of programs, greater subject expertise, broadening of application areas, greater emphasis on management, and greater emphasis on research.[36] This list suggests that library education programs in the future may be more supportive of subject specialization, including specialization in sci-tech librarianship. There is increasing interest among the specialized library and information professional associations, such as the Special Libraries Association, in playing a greater part in the accreditation process.[37] The intent is to help shape library school programs to be more responsive to the demands of specialized settings.

PROSPECT

> One important fact which librarians can learn from the scientists is the importance of being able to adapt old concepts to altered conditions.
>
> *Charles Harvey Brown, 1953*[38]

Education for sci-tech librarianship will continue to be concerned with information sources and services, but must be responsive to "altered conditions." To suggest directions for further development of educational programs for sci-tech librarianship, the remainder of this paper briefly considers three themes: new roles, new information sources, and scientific literacy.

New Roles

Because the sci-tech librarian is concerned with providing information needed for research and development, changes in the ways in which research and development are undertaken may lead to the possibility of new roles for sci-tech librarians. For example, Neway demonstrates the role that the information specialist can play as a team member in a variety of research settings.[39] As team research is increasingly conducted via international computer networks,[40] the librarian must identify ways to contribute to the process.

In addition to providing new services, librarians will be involved increasingly as designers of systems. As Simon has observed, "design . . . is the core of all professional training; it is the principal mark that distinguishes the professions from the sciences."[41] He argues that each profession must discover a science of design which can serve as the basis of instruction in professional schools. As just one example of the types of systems which librarians may help to design, Brittain identifies expert systems.[42] In particular he suggests that librarians are likely to play a role in the knowledge acquisition phase of expert system development. Work in expert systems moves beyond bibliography to a new generation of information services that are concerned with the transfer and use of information in scientific research and development, among other applications.

New Information Sources

Observers of the role of the supercomputer in scientific research have suggested that it challenges scientists to ask new questions, because they now have a tool suitable for answering them. Likewise the proliferation of nonbibliographic databases-numeric, factual, and full text-offers a wide array of new information sources. Even where the same source exists in printed form, its machine-readable counterpart may make it possible to answer a much wider range of questions because of the flexibility and speed with which the contents can be searched. Although sci-tech librarians have extensive experience with bibliographic databases and the range of questions they can answer, the current challenge is to conceptualize new uses for the entire sci-tech electronic library that is becoming available.

Scientific Literacy

In a report entitled *Into the Information Age*, the authors suggested that one could identify three eras in sci-tech information.[43] The first, discipline oriented, emphasizes traditional means of dissemination of information from scientist to scientist. The next era, beginning with World War II, is termed mission-oriented, with information from a variety of disciplines used to accomplish some goal. The third era, beginning in the late 1960s, is termed problem-oriented, recognizing the increasing societal need for dealing with complex and wide ranging issues (e.g., energy, environment, health and using information for problem solution. In the third era sci-tech information needs to be augmented with societal information; legal, social, political, and economic considerations also figure in decision making. Because such information lies outside what is traditionally thought of as sci-tech, education for sci-tech librarianship cannot be limited to the sci-tech literature alone.

Just as sci-tech librarians must take a broader view and be concerned with societal information, all librarians should have some level of understanding of sci-tech information in the interest of promoting scientific literacy. This plea is not new. In 1959 Bonn reviewed the role of school, public, and college librarians in providing science information and concluded: "In my view it is of course axiomatic that *all* students in library school should receive at least one dose of sci-tech literature. It will be good for every one of them!"[44] But there is an increased urgency in the concern for scientific literacy as we confront the problems of the third era. According to Miller, scientific literacy is "the ability of the individual to read about, comprehend, and express an opinion on scientific matters."[45] In addition to understanding the norms and methods of science and having a knowledge of scientific constructs, everyone needs an awareness of the impact of science and technology on society and the policy choices that must inevitably emerge. Thus the challenge to library education is not limited to developing stronger programs for sci-tech librarianship, but must encompass equipping all librarians with the knowledge necessary to promote scientific literacy.

NOTES

1. Hanson, C. W. *Introduction to science-information work.* London: Aslib; 1971: p. 1.

2. Brown, Charles Harvey. Librarianship and the sciences. In: Shores, Louis, ed. *Challenges to librarianship.* Tallahassee, FL: Florida State University; 1953: p. 82.

3. Friedel, J. H. *Training for Librarianship: library work as a career.* Philadelphia: J. B. Lippincott; 1921.

3a. Troutman, Ray. *A history of the School of Library Service, Columbia University.* New York: Columbia University Press; 1954: p. 48.

4. Orton, Floyd Emory. A preparatory program for science and technology librarians. *Special Libraries.* 35(1): 11-15; 1944 January.

5. Voigt, Melvin J., ed. Education for special librarianship. *Library Quarterly.* 24(1): 1-20; 1954 January.

6. Bonn, George S. Library school courses in science-technology literature. In: *Science, technical libraries and the education of special librarians.* Philadelphia: Drexel Institute of Technology; 1959; p. 30.

7. Williams, Robert V.; Zachert, Martha Jane K. Specialization in library education: a review of the trends and issues. *Journal of Education for Library and Information Science.* 26(4): 230; 1986 Spring.

8. Rossiter, Margaret W. Women and the history of scientific communication. *Journal of Library History, Philosophy and Comparative Librarianship.* 21(1): 49: 1986 Winter.

9. Cohan, Leonard; Craven, Kenneth. *Science information personnel: the new profession of information combining science, librarianship, and foreign language.* New York: Modern Language Association of America; 1961.

10. *Summary proceedings of the Georgia Tech conference on training science information specialists, October 12-13, 1961.* Atlanta, GA: Georgia Institute of Technology; 1962.

11. Goldwyn, A. J.; Rees, Alan M., eds. *The education of science information personnel-1964; proceedings of an invitational conference.* Cleveland, OH: Center for Documentation and Communication Research, School of Library Science, Western Reserve University; 1965.

12. *International conference on education for scientific information work.* The Hague: Federation Internationale de Documentation (FID); 1967 September.

13. Welt, Isaac D. Editorial: information science-science information. *American Documentation.* 15(4): 249; 1964 October.

14. Haselbauer, Kathleen. The making of a science librarian. *Science & Technology Libraries.* 4(3/4): 111-116; 1984 Spring/Summer.

15. Voigt, Melvin J. Scientific and technical librarianship. *Library Quarterly.* 24(1): 13; 1954 January.

16. Hunt, Judith Wallen. Science librarianship. *Science*. 104(2695): 172; 1946 August 23.

17. Rossiter, p. 39.

18. Fasick, Adele M. Library and information science students. *Library Trends*. 34(4): 607-621; 1986 Spring.

19. Dewey, Barbara I. Science background required—others need not apply: a study of the science librarian hiring crisis. In: *ASIS '86 proceedings*. Medford, NJ: Learned Information; 1986: p. 64-68.

20. Bonn, George S. Training for activity in scientific documentation work. In: *Proceedings of the International Conference on Scientific Information*. Washington, DC: National Academy of Sciences-National Research Council; 1959: p. 1441-1488.

21. Owens, Elizabeth W. A survey of special library education. *Special Libraries*. 51(6): 288-293; 1960 July-August.

22. Ripin, Arley L.; Kasman, Dorothy. Education for special librarianship: a survey of courses offered in accredited programs. *Special Libraries*. 67(11): 504-509; 1976 November.

23. Mellott, Constance M. Courses for special librarianship offered in A.L.A. accredited programs and implications for the education of science/technology librarians. *Science & Technology Libraries*. 1(3): 13-20; 1981 Spring.

24. Shera, Jesse H. An educational program for special librarians. *Journal of Education for Librarianship*. 1(3): 125; 1961 Winter.

25. Voigt, Scientific and technical librarianship, p. 9-13.

26. Goldwyn and Rees, p. 18.

27. Science information courses initiated at Georgia Tech. *Library Journal*. 88(12): 2473-2474; 1963 June 15.

28. Wiggins, Gary. The Indiana University chemical information specialist program: training the library user and the librarian. *Science & Technology Libraries*. 1(3): 5-11; 1981 Spring.

29. Dosa, Marta. The education of environmental information specialists. In: Jackson, Eugene B., ed. *Special librarianship: a new reader*. Metuchen, NJ: Scarecrow Press; 1980: p. 133-139.

30. Schur, H.; Saunders, W. L. *Education and training for scientific and technological library and information work*. London: Her Majesty's Stationery Office; 1968: p. 66-67.

31. Bonn, Library school courses in science-technology literature, p. 24-33.

32. Matarazzo, James M. *Library problems in science and technology*. New York: R. R. Bowker; 1971.

33. Wilson, Conception S. Teaching science bibliography: from classroom to market-place. *Journal of Education for Librarianship*. 23(2): 125-136; 1982 Fall.

34. Lenfest, Donna D.; Goldhor, Herbert. Interdepartmental training program for science information specialists at the University of Illinois. *Journal of Education for Librarianship*. 12(2): 84-91; 1971 Fall.

35. Martin, Jess A. University of Tennessee postgraduate training program for science librarians: a six-year review. *Bulletin of the Medical Library Association*. 61(4): 396-399; 1973 October.

36. Hayes, Robert M. Accreditation. *Library Trends*. 34(4): 537-559; 1986 Spring.

37. Arterbery, Vivian J. Accreditation: a blueprint for action. *Special Libraries*. 77(4): 230-234; 1986 Fall.

38. Brown, p. 87.

39. Newly, Julie M. *Information specialist as team player in the research process*. Westport, CT: Greenwood Press; 1985.

40. Dobrov, G. M.; Randolph, R. H.; Rauch, W. D. New options for team research via international computer networks. *Scientometrics*. 1(5-6): 387-404; 1979 August.

41. Simon, Herbert A. *The sciences of the artificial*. 2d ed. Cambridge, MA: MIT Press; 1981: p. 129.

42. Brittain, Michael. Implications for LIS educational of recent developments in expert systems. *Information Processing & Management*. 23(2): 139-152; 1987.

43. Arthur D. Little, Inc. *Into the information age: a perspective for federal action on information*. Chicago: American Library Association; 1978.

44. Bonn, Library school courses in science-technology literature, p. 33.

45. Miller, Jon D. Scientific literacy: a conceptual and empirical review. *Daedalus*. 112(2): 30; 1983 Spring.

SPECIAL PAPER

Statistical Data for Stand-Alone Science/Engineering Libraries in the United States and Canada 1984/1985

Emerson Hilker

BACKGROUND

This compilation of statistical data represents a project undertaken by the ACRL Science and Technology Section to compare the operations of significant academic science/engineering libraries in the United States and Canada. The Task Force on Comparison of Science/Engineering Libraries met at the Midwinter and Annual ALA Conferences in 1986 to examine the results from completed questionnaires returned by participating libraries during the 1985/1986 academic year. Data from each questionnaire was assembled into comparative tables and eventually was entered into an IBM-PC.

The tables reproduced here disclose data on physical characteristics, clientele, collections, expenditures, personnel, and public ser-

---

Emerson Hilker is Head of the Physical Sciences and Engineering Division, Oklahoma State University, Library, Stillwater, OK 74078.

vices statistics for circulation, interlibrary loan, reference, library instruction, database searching, fees, and fines. Summary information from a professional salary survey is also presented.

The questionnaire utilized for this project is based on the model developed by the Editorial Board for *Annual Statistics of Medical School Libraries in the United States and Canada*, now in its 8th edition for 1984/1985. With certain appropriate revisions, this instrument has enabled the Task Force to discover a sizable quantity of information about a group of strong, sci/tech libraries.

In future years, as the number of participants increase and the quality of the questionnaire improves, the Task Force hopes to create a useful guide to the management, operations and services of this type of library.

MEMBERSHIP

Task Force members designed the project initially to include only a subset of the strong scientific collections. The committee was motivated by the desire to have significant results available within a relatively short time frame. Project planners formulated the list of potential participants on the basis of similarity so that the data assembled could be more usefully related.

With this in mind, the list of ARL libraries was examined to identify highly centralized science/engineering collections. ARL institutions whose scientific and engineering collections were housed together in a "stand-alone" or "free-standing" unit became immediate candidates. To expand the group of survey members but still retain similarities of operation, the committee extended the definition for inclusion to encompass science/engineering collections housed together as a separate unit in a main library building alongside humanities and/or social science collections.

Other variants were added, including institutions owning separate but co-equal science and engineering libraries or physical science and life science libraries. Furthermore, inclusion is permitted in those cases where small branches or reading rooms report to a main science/ engineering unit. Several strong sci/tech libraries not on the ARL membership list were also contacted.

By the end of 1985, 37 institutions (32 US, 5 Canadian) had been sent questionnaires inviting their participation in the survey. Of that group, 22 libraries sent in completed questionnaires. Of the remaining 15, all but one library responded favorably to the concept. Five institutions had hoped to submit their data for the first edition but for varying reasons could not meet the deadline. Six institutions are now in various stages of merging their collections into a new stand-alone facility and expect to submit data in the next edition.

Two institutions felt their libraries did not fit the definition. Two libraries have not responded to initial queries on their intentions. One institution that returned a completed questionnaire did not segregate data for their sci/tech collections and could therefore not be included in the tables.

The list of participating institutions with the name and phone number of the contact person and a library code precedes the statistical data.

For the next edition, perhaps years hence, the Task Force intends to expand inclusion to institutions presently candidates for ARL membership and colleges or polytechnic institutes with notable sci/tech holdings. There will also be plans laid to contact centralized science collections in ARL institutions to determine how their operations might be both represented and contrasted in the compilation.

TABLES

Institutions are arranged in alphabetical order throughout the compilation. In many instances libraries were not able to submit data for certain categories. In such cases the symbol "U" so indicates. Where two institutions have separate science and engineering libraries, each unit is listed separately. However, when an average value for a category is computed, the individual units are combined.

Library Characteristics

Table 1 describes the physical facility including the branch libraries, if any. Data supplied comprises the year established; the type of physical facility [stand-alone (S), housed in main building with other units (M), or sharing a building with academic departments (A)]; subject fields covered; floor space; seating capacity; individual or group study rooms; number of branches; etc.

For the main units, the average floor space encompasses 43,000 square feet, increasing to 50,000 square feet when the branch libraries are included. Seating capacity averages 536 places; less than half report faculty study rooms; groups study rooms are only sparsely available.

Library and Automated Functions

Table 2 describes the location of nonpublic service library functions and availability of automated services. With the exception of bindery preparation, nonpublic services are performed centrally.

Functions reported comprise acquisitions, cataloging, binding, serials check-in, interlibrary loan, automation and administration.

Automated operations listed embrace acquisitions, authority control, cataloging, circulation, online public catalog, public access terminals, serials check-in, serials control, interlibrary loan, and other.

The member libraries demonstrate by this report a substantial degree of automation in all categories excepting public access and serials.

Primary Clientele

Table 3 analyzes the primary academic clientele served by each institution, incorporating an individual breakdown by department. The average number of faculty, undergraduate and graduate students served by these institutions are 489, 4592, and 1397 respectively.

In Table A, mean values are provided for subject categories where sufficient data is available.

The departmental analysis becomes less clear as new academic programs emerge. The "Other" category contains significant numbers of students and faculty in cross disciplines.

Library Collections—Total Volumes

Table 4 presents the number of volumes or volume equivalents added and withdrawn, in off-site storage, and the resulting totals at the end of the fiscal year for each institution.

The mean for number of printed volumes added just exceeds 12,000 while total volumes averages nearly 320,000.

Library Collections Serials

Table 5 accounts for the total number of serial titles (dead and current) in each library and provides a separate aggregate for current subscriptions, whether received by purchase, gift, or exchange.

The average number of current titles in survey libraries amounts to one-half of the average total in the collections (4,700 vs. 8,800).

Expenditures

Table 6 supplies U.S. dollar values for expenditures in eight budgetary classifications: monographs, serials, audiovisuals, binding, salaries, staff development, utilities and other.

Expenditures for monographs in these libraries stands at 22% of the total acquisitions budget versus 78% for serials.

The means for binding and salaries exceed 52,000 and 335,000, respectively.

Expenditures by Subject

For those libraries able to segregate acquisitions expenditures by subject, the mean values for printed materials are as shown in Table B. For further information see Table 7.

Personnel

Table 8 tallies the number of full-time equivalents in professional, support, and hourly wage brackets.

For the professional category, the average institution staffs 6.5 FTE. In the support classification, the FTE value is 12; and in the hourly wage category, 31 FTE.

Building Use and Access Hours

Table 9 reports total attendance for the year, number of hours during the week the library is open, and the weekly sum of hours when at least one library professional is on duty followed by the total man-hours of reference service available to patrons.

For those libraries counting attendance, the average number of persons entering or leaving the library approaches 620,000. These libraries are open an average of 107 hours per week; at least one reference librarian is on duty roughly half the time (55 hours per week). The mean of total reference hours is 100.

Circulation Periods

Table 10 displays circulation periods for journals, monographs, documents, microforms, and audiovisuals.

Loan periods are indicated in terms of days or fractions thereof. The letter "N" is inserted where materials may be used only within the building.

Collection Use and Interlibrary Loan

Table 11 represents usage figures for circulation separated into external, closed reserve, in-house and photocopies (number of prints).

Appropriate averages for these categories are 61,000, 21,000, 210,000, and 909,000 respectively.

In addition, this table furnishes the number of loans or photocopies borrowed from other libraries and the number of lending and filled requests for other libraries.

On average the number of items borrowed is not much more than 1/3 of the total of those lent.

Information Services and Library Instruction

Table 12 shows yearly activity in reference services and library instruction. Statistics on directional questions are so variable and scattered that averages would be meaningless. Reference questions appear to be more widely and carefully calculated. The mean for that service is nearly 18,000 per year.

The average number of tours and lectures provided in member libraries is surprisingly close. The standard for sessions is 25 and 31, respectively; and the number of students attending, 390 and 431, respectively.

Database Accesses

Table 13 classifies database searches according to the following files accessed: Agricola, Biosis, CA Search, Compendex, Conference Papers, EI Meetings, Inspec, Mathfile, Medline, NTIS, Scisearch, and Other.

The average number of searches conducted each year is 813, but a few libraries are clustered at the top of the range; i.e., 30% of the institutions account for 75% of the searching activity.

Types of Searches

Table 14 provides information to further refine database searching activity. Data is shown for end-user searching, active SDI profiles, RLIN/OCLC searches, and free or low-cost vendor searches at the reference desk.

Fees for Service

Table 15 indicates what fees are assessed for photocopying, reference/research services, and database searching.

If the service is not available the letter "n" is indicated. A variable fee is denoted by the letter "V." A "0" symbolizes a free service.

Penalty Fees—Maximum Overdue Fees

Table 16 represents maximum overdue fees charged for journals, monographs, government documents, microforms, audiovisuals, and reserves.

Zeros indicate that no overdue fee is assessed. An "N" describes a format that does not circulate. When there is no maximum fee, an "NM" is inserted.

Penalty Fees — Per Day Fees

Table 17 delineates the per day fees for overdue materials as in Table 16. Where the maximum fee is identical to the per day charge, the letter "S" is indicated. N is displayed for noncirculating formats.

The tables also show processing fees for lost books and the method by which the price of the lost book is determined (average index price or original cost).

Salary Survey

Nine of the Unit Heads are designated as assistant directors. This additional appointment does not necessarily mean a higher salary. The average salary for ADs and non-ADs is very close.

The salary questionnaire asked each institution to supply:

1. Whether the Head of the Science/Engineering Library also assumes an administrative position at the Assistant Director level;
2. the annual salary of the Head;
3. the average annual salary of Public Services Librarians in the Science/Engineering Library;
4. the average annual salary of Technical Services Librarians in the Science/Engineering Library;
5. the minimum published salary offered to an entry level librarian in the Science/Engineering Library.

The results are depicted in Table C in four categories: highest, lowest, mid-point, and average.

TABLE A

	Faculty	Undergrads	Graduates
Mathematics	46	400	60
Computer Science	18	468	108
Physics	44	117	79
Chemistry	35	215	129
Earth Sciences	21	87	65
Biological Sciences	61	489	166
Engineering	117	1,995	521

TABLE B

	Monographs	Serials	Totals
Mathematics	11,694	49,517	57,366
Computer Science	9,028	14,334	21,571
Astronomy	4,116	14,545	15,752
Physics	11,672	65,096	70,879
Chemistry	15,399	103,855	111,466
Earth Sciences	11,343	30,747	40,210
Biological Sciences	21,674	87,543	91,728
Engineering	33,369	102,445	121,754

TABLE C

	Highest	Lowest	Mid-pt	Average
Head	50,500	25,912	35,106	35,868
Public Services	36,254	18,000	25,969	25,647
Technical Services (only 4)	29,400	16,500	18,166	20,292
Entry Level	28,583	14,880	17,900	19,243

TABLE 1.
LIBRARY CHARACTERISTICS - MAIN AND BRANCH LIBRARIES

Lib	Year Est	Phy Fac	Sub Covd	MAIN Square Footage	Seat Cap	Study I	Study G	#	BRANCHES (cumulative) Square Footage	Seat Cap	SR I	SR G
ASU	1983	S	10	89,000	1,050	58	22	0	0	0	0	0
CIT	1983	M	9	8,927	241	0	0	7	15,397	94	0	0
MSU	1955	M	6	51,116	1,578	0	6	7	28,641	441	0	0
NWU	1977	S	8	50,000	450	0	3	2	4,322	38	0	0
SIU	1955	M	4	27,179	260	37	0	0	0	0	0	0
SUN	1949	A	10	76,350	950	58	6	3	19,661	489	0	2
UAL/E	1962	A	9	7,300	85	0	0	0	0	0	0	0
UAL/S	1964	A	U	10,000	120	0	0	0	0	0	0	0
UAB	1964	M	26	35,000	346	11	0	3	7,768	69	0	0
UAR	1963	S	35	122,710	1,095	97	13	0	0	0	0	0
UCR	1961	A	11	5,335	55	0	0	0	0	0	0	0
UCS	1964	A	11	17,197	149	0	0	1	1,000	12	0	0
UGL	1968	S	U	75,780	788	159	1	0	0	0	0	0
UKL	1954	A	7	25,318	207	0	1	3	14,564	230	0	0
UMA/E	1907	M	5	9,327	214	0	0	0	0	0	0	0
UMA/S	1906	S	12	29,224	587	0	1	0	0	0	0	0
UMN	1985	M	4	U	U	0	0	2	8,800	155	0	0
USC	1969	S	8	24,200	240	0	1	0	0	0	0	0
UVA	1975	A	6	31,002	365	0	0	4	9,495	139	0	0
WSU	1952	S	18	88,531	830	5	6	2	13,200	220	0	0
WAY	1971	S	9	42,000	700	16	27	0	0	0	0	0
YAL	1966	A	5	24,537	204	0	0	5	20,145	187	0	0
YOR	1970	S	8	13,600	200	0	0	0	0	0	0	0

U Not reported

TABLE 2.
LIBRARY CHARACTERISTICS - LIBRARY AND AUTOMATED FUNCTIONS

LIBRARY FUNCTIONS

Library	Acq	Cat	Bind	Ser	ILL	Auto	Adm
ASU	yes	yes	yes	yes	yes	yes	yes
CIT	yes	yes	yes	yes	yes	yes	yes
MSU	yes	yes	no	yes	yes	yes	no
NWU	yes	yes	no	yes	yes	yes	yes
SIU	yes	yes	yes	yes	yes	yes	yes
SUN	yes	yes	yes	yes	no	yes	no
UAL/E	yes	yes	no	yes	yes	yes	yes
UAL/S	yes	yes	yes	yes	yes	yes	yes
UAB	yes	yes	yes	yes	yes	yes	yes
UAR	yes	yes	yes	yes	yes	yes	no
UCR	yes	yes	no	no	yes	yes	no
UCS	yes	yes	no	no	yes	yes	yes
UGL	yes	yes	no	yes	yes	yes	no
UKL	no	yes	no	yes	yes	yes	yes
UMA/E	yes	yes	yes	yes	yes	yes	yes
UMA/S	yes	yes	yes	yes	yes	yes	yes
UMN	yes	yes	no	yes	yes	yes	no
USC	yes	yes	no	yes	yes	yes	no
UVA	yes	yes	no	yes	no	yes	yes
WSU	yes	yes	no	no	yes	yes	yes
WAY	yes	yes	no	no	no	yes	yes
YAL	no	yes	no	no	no	no	no
YOR	yes	yes	no	yes	yes	yes	no

AUTOMATED FUNCTIONS

Lib	Acq	Auth	Cat	Circ	OPAC	PA	S Ch	S Cn	ILL	Other
ASU	no	no	no	yes	yes	yes	no	no	no	no
CIT	yes	no	yes	no	yes	no	no	no	yes	no
MSU	yes	no	yes	yes	no	no	yes	no	yes	no
NWU	yes	yes	yes	yes	yes	yes	yes	yes	no	no
SIU	no	no	yes	yes	yes	no	no	no	yes	yes
SUN	no	no	yes	yes	no	no	no	no	yes	no
UAL/E	no	no	yes	no	no	no	no	no	yes	no
UAL/S	no	yes	yes	yes	yes	yes	no	no	yes	no
UAB	yes	yes	yes	yes	yes	yes	no	no	no	no
UAR	no	no	no	yes	no	yes	no	no	no	no
UCR	yes	yes	yes	yes	yes	yes	yes	yes	yes	no
UCS	no	no	yes	no	no	no	yes	yes	yes	no
UGL	yes	no	yes	yes	yes	no	yes	yes	yes	no
UKL	yes	yes	yes	yes	no	no	no	yes	no	yes
UMA/E	yes	yes	yes	yes	no	no	yes	no	no	no
UMA/S	yes	yes	yes	yes	yes	no	no	yes	yes	no
UMN	yes	no	yes	no	no	no	no	no	yes	no
USC	yes	no	yes	yes	yes	yes	yes	yes	no	no
UVA	yes	no	yes	yes	no	yes	no	no	yes	no
WSU	yes	yes	yes	yes	yes	yes	no	no	yes	no
WAY	yes	no	no	no	no	no	no	no	no	no
YAL	no	no	yes	yes	no	yes	no	no	yes	no
YOR	yes	yes	yes	yes	yes	yes	no	no	yes	no

TABLE 3.
PRIMARY CLIENTELE

Lib	MATHEMATICS				COMPUTER SCIENCE			
	Fac	Und	Grad	Total	Fac	Und	Grad	Total
ASU	46	199	38	283	23	850	225	1,098
CIT	27	22	25	74	4	0	37	41
MSU	98	423	102	623	25	770	96	891
NWU	32	91	40	163	0	0	0	0
SIU	U	U	U	U	12	584	60	656
SUN	39	139	69	247	8	140	113	261
UAL/E	0	0	0	0	6	139	29	174
UAL/S	41	65	17	123	6	359	23	388
UAB	47	0	18	65	21	0	74	95
UAR	57	1,696	63	1,816	15	130	36	181
UCR	21	113	25	159	0	206	42	248
UCS	107	286	106	499	22	214	65	301
UGL	57	106	35	198	11	900	90	1,001
UKL	37	2,540	56	2,633	14	919	316	1,249
UMA/E	0	0	0	0	0	0	0	0
UMA/S	32	U	U	32	48	U	U	48
UMN	87	172	134	393	23	601	265	889
USC	34	200	300	534	15	100	150	265
UVA	27	109	47	183	14	0	0	14
WSU	21	1,063	37	1,121	13	461	48	522
WAY	44	33	33	110	53	375	90	518
YAL	26	38	45	109	20	20	73	113
YOR	U	310	0	310	U	721	0	721

Lib	ASTRONOMY				PHYSICS			
	Fac	Und	Grad	Total	Fac	Und	Grad	Total
ASU	0	0	0	0	36	104	70	210
CIT	27	6	19	52	76	128	126	330
MSU	0	0	0	0	130	150	100	380
NWU	0	0	0	0	30	30	55	115
SIU	U	U	U	U	U	U	U	U
SUN	0	0	0	0	22	26	60	108
UAL/E	0	0	0	0	0	0	0	0
UAL/S	0	0	0	0	20	14	21	55
UAB	0	0	0	0	42	0	59	101
UAR	12	308	16	336	39	461	59	559
UCR	0	0	0	0	20	200	65	285
UCS	22	0	0	22	95	108	108	311
UGL	2	7	0	9	30	36	29	95
UKL	24	985	68	1,077	0	0	0	0
UMA/E	0	0	0	0	0	0	0	0
UMA/S	4	U	U	4	47	U	U	47
UMN	11	33	10	54	49	122	116	287
USC	3	20	0	23	25	150	225	400
UVA	13	15	16	44	42	38	71	151
WSU	0	0	0	0	14	241	42	297
WAY	0	0	0	0	35	85	60	180
YAL	8	0	13	21	33	50	104	187
YOR	U	0	0	U	U	46	52	98

U   Not reported

TABLE 3 (continued)

Lib	BIOLOGICAL SCIENCES				ENGINEERING			
	Fac	Und	Grad	Total	Fac	Und	Grad	Total
ASU	58	633	117	808	206	4,712	1,100	6,018
CIT	62	41	65	168	114	338	414	866
MSU	185	1,178	386	1,749	124	4,060	443	4,627
NWU	43	70	69	182	130	1,286	784	2,200
SIU	U	U	U	U	70	2,462	103	2,635
SUN	30	75	77	182	88	2,630	410	3,128
UAL/E	0	0	0	0	104	1,950	176	2,230
UAL/S	33	257	41	331	0	0	0	0
UAB	56	0	141	197	109	2,181	382	2,672
UAR	54	733	84	871	184	1,830	450	2,464
UCR	0	0	0	0	0	0	0	0
UCS	0	0	0	0	126	1,246	285	1,657
UGL	163	621	297	1,081	0	0	0	0
UKL	64	1,564	467	2,095	73	1,826	641	2,540
UMA/E	0	0	0	0	79	1,299	297	1,675
UMA/S	51	U	U	51	0	0	0	0
UMN	0	0	0	0	160	4,458	832	5,450
USC	36	220	350	606	182	1,200	1,600	2,982
UVA	32	263	60	355	158	1,411	556	2,125
WSU	51	789	147	987	83	896	204	1,183
WAY	29	512	194	735	68	2,079	596	2,743
YAL	30	100	95	225	39	49	104	192
YOR	U	282	65	347	0	0	0	0

Lib	CHEMISTRY				EARTH SCIENCES			
	Fac	Und	Grad	Total	Fac	Und	Grad	Total
ASU	33	176	97	306	13	80	69	162
CIT	43	32	162	237	43	11	81	135
MSU	34	199	197	430	19	115	51	185
NWU	30	120	115	265	12	6	33	51
SIU	U	U	U	U	U	U	U	U
SUN	27	70	127	224	28	37	50	115
UAL/E	0	0	0	0	0	0	0	0
UAL/S	17	72	41	130	20	82	55	157
UAB	44	0	146	190	18	0	89	107
UAR	52	745	116	913	29	133	82	244
UCR	16	46	60	122	14	50	72	136
UCS	110	113	152	375	0	0	0	0
UGL	36	150	80	266	51	95	93	239
UKL	19	915	160	1,094	11	399	83	493
UMA/E	0	0	0	0	0	0	0	0
UMA/S	30	U	U	30	17	U	U	17
UMN	41	89	186	316	23	39	66	128
USC	24	175	250	449	17	110	170	297
UVA	24	200	99	323	31	70	61	162
WSU	28	509	128	665	10	211	56	277
WAY	29	140	145	314	5	33	14	52
YAL	28	15	157	200	24	30	45	99
YOR	U	100	34	134	U	68	0	68

U Not reported

TABLE 3 (continued)

Lib	AGRICULTURE				MEDICINE			
	Fac	Und	Grad	Total	Fac	Und	Grad	Total
ASU	21	187	44	252	0	0	0	0
CIT	0	0	0	0	0	0	0	0
MSU	350	2,410	737	3,497	308	0	812	1,120
NWU	0	0	0	0	0	0	0	0
SIU	52	678	131	861	43	0	72	115
SUN	0	0	0	0	0	0	0	0
UAL/E	0	0	0	0	0	0	0	0
UAL/S	0	0	0	0	0	0	0	0
UAB	83	819	246	1,148	0	0	0	0
UAR	48	579	233	860	0	0	0	0
UCR	0	0	0	0	0	0	0	0
UCS	0	0	0	0	0	0	0	0
UGL	415	1,055	296	1,766	0	0	0	0
UKL	0	0	0	0	0	0	0	0
UMA/E	0	0	0	0	0	0	0	0
UMA/S	0	0	0	0	0	0	0	0
UMN	0	0	0	0	0	0	0	0
USC	0	0	0	0	0	0	0	0
UVA	0	0	0	0	0	0	0	0
WSU	73	758	240	1,071	6	0	51	57
WAY	0	0	0	0	0	0	0	0
YAL	0	0	0	0	0	0	0	0
YOR	0	0	0	0	0	0	0	0

Lib	NURSING				VETERINARY MEDICINE			
	Fac	Und	Grad	Total	Fac	Und	Grad	Total
ASU	75	677	204	956	0	0	0	0
CIT	0	0	0	0	0	0	0	0
MSU	48	483	60	591	185	421	395	1,001
NWU	0	0	0	0	0	0	0	0
SIU	0	0	0	0	0	0	0	0
SUN	0	0	0	0	0	0	0	0
UAL/E	0	0	0	0	0	0	0	0
UAL/S	0	0	0	0	0	0	0	0
UAB	0	0	0	0	0	0	0	0
UAR	0	0	0	0	0	0	0	0
UCR	0	0	0	0	0	0	0	0
UCS	0	0	0	0	0	0	0	0
UGL	0	0	0	0	135	85	120	340
UKL	0	0	0	0	0	0	0	0
UMA/E	0	0	0	0	0	0	0	0
UMA/S	0	0	0	0	0	0	0	0
UMN	0	0	0	0	0	0	0	0
USC	0	0	0	0	0	0	0	0
UVA	0	0	0	0	0	0	0	0
WSU	0	0	0	0	66	296	294	656
WAY	90	514	380	984	0	0	0	0
YAL	0	0	0	0	0	0	0	0
YOR	0	0	0	0	0	0	0	0

TABLE 3 (continued)

	HOME ECONOMICS				OTHER (Totals)			
Lib	Fac	Und	Grad	Total	Fac	Und	Grad	Total
ASU	14	435	29	478	15	126	42	183
CIT	0	0	0	0	470	236	0	706
MSU	76	1,018	109	1,203	14	11	60	85
NWU	0	0	0	0	0	0	0	0
SIU	U	U	U	U	115	883	318	1,316
SUN	0	0	0	0	0	0	0	0
UAL/E	0	0	0	0	0	0	0	0
UAL/S	33	474	54	561	0	0	0	0
UAB	24	414	50	488	284	4,645	527	5,456
UAR	21	357	147	525	0	0	0	0
UCR	0	0	0	0	33	51	76	160
UCS	0	0	0	0	16	0	0	16
UGL	56	715	84	855	150	545	91	786
UKL	0	0	0	0	21	412	202	635
UMA/E	0	0	0	0	0	0	0	0
UMA/S	0	0	0	0	0	0	0	0
UMN	0	0	0	0	35	332	49	416
USC	0	0	0	0	0	0	0	0
UVA	0	0	0	0	38	350	74	462
WSU	3	207	12	222	32	421	71	524
WAY	37	300	80	417	0	0	0	0
YAL	0	0	0	0	31	50	202	283
YOR	0	0	0	0	U	467	3	470

	GRAND TOTALS			
Library	Faculty	Under	Graduate	Total
Arizona State University	540	8,179	2,035	10,754
California Inst of Technology	866	814	929	2,609
Michigan State University	1,596	11,238	3,548	16,382
Northwestern University	277	1,603	1,096	2,976
Southern Ill U @ Carbondale	292	4,607	684	5,583
SUNY - Buffalo	242	3,117	906	4,265
University of Alabama/Eng	110	2,089	205	2,404
University of Alabama/Science	170	1,323	252	1,745
University of Alberta	728	8,059	1,732	10,519
University of Arizona	511	6,972	1,286	8,769
University of Cal @ Riverside	104	666	340	1,110
University of Cal @ San Diego	498	1,967	716	3,181
Univ of Georgia Libraries	1,106	4,315	1,215	6,636
University of Kansas	263	9,560	1,993	11,816
University of Manitoba/Eng	79	1,299	297	1,675
University of Manitoba/Science	229	U	U	229
University of Minnesota	429	5,846	1,658	7,933
Univ of Southern California	336	2,175	3,045	5,556
University of Virginia	379	2,456	984	3,819
Washington State University	400	5,852	1,330	7,582
Wayne State University	390	4,071	1,592	6,053
Yale University	239	352	838	1,429
York University	U	1,994	154	2,148

U Not reported

TABLE 4.
LIBRARY COLLECTIONS - TOTAL VOLUMES

Library	PRINT Added	With-Drawn	Off-site Storage	Total
Arizona State Univ	15,000	U	0	285,000
Cal Inst of Technology	6,476	508	0	235,000
Michigan State Univ	22,183	3,663	100,000	583,943
Northwestern University	6,034	U	36,760	258,649
S Ill @ Carbondale	8,212	100	0	338,100
SUNY - Buffalo	10,832	738	0	364,561
Univ of Alabama/Eng	2,277	0	0	69,109
Univ of Alabama/Science	3,819	0	0	98,762
University of Alberta	19,100	0	0	347,100
University of Arizona	21,865	0	0	382,445
Univ of Cal @ Riverside	4,443	348	13,902	92,859
Univ of Cal @ San Diego	7,831	1,432	0	138,518
Univ of Georgia Lib	20,000	0	0	526,000
University of Kansas	20,866	314	0	571,546
Univ of Manitoba/Eng	2,246	390	6,022	38,070
Univ of Manitoba/Science	6,092	426	0	115,591
University of Minnesota	U	U	U	U
Univ of Southern Cal	10,600	1,000	12,000	224,000
University of Virginia	10,807	2,881	U	302,002
Wash State University	15,787	1,773	29,213	447,580
Wayne State University	11,399	203	0	334,823
Yale University	10,830	1,616	97,000	498,436
York University	5,446	29	0	90,880

Lib	MICROFORM Added	With-Drawn	Off-Site	Total	AUDIOVISUAL Added	With-Drawn	Off-Site	Total
ASU	100,000	0	0	465,000	0	0	0	0
CIT	7,500	0	0	220,000	0	0	0	0
MSU	0	0	0	5,826	0	0	0	25
NWU	U	0	0	U	0	0	0	0
SIU	U	0	0	U	0	0	0	0
SUN	38,225	326	0	1,260,264	325	U	120	1,345
UAL/E	0	0	0	0	0	0	0	0
UAL/S	10,000	0	0	190,000	0	0	0	0
UAB	700	0	0	30,000	0	0	0	0
UAR	100,854	0	0	1,129,590	0	0	0	0
UCR	844	35	0	15,839	U	0	0	0
UCS	22,821	0	0	68,570	0	0	0	0
UGL	U	0	0	250,000	U	0	0	485,523
UKL	41,121	0	0	189,280	0	0	0	0
UMA/E	908	0	0	13,084	0	0	0	17
UMA/S	33	0	0	1,146	0	0	0	2
UMN	U	U	U	U	U	U	U	U
USC	1,200	0	0	22,000	0	0	0	0
UVA	0	0	0	5,039	0	0	0	0
WSU	70,292	2,636	0	594,611	U	U	U	U
WAY	21,302	0	0	80,498	0	0	0	0
YAL	2,589	0	0	185,500	4,670	1,145	0	173,855
YOR	673	0	0	27,512	0	0	0	0

U   Not reported

TABLE 5.
LIBRARY COLLECTIONS - SERIALS

	TOTAL IN COLLECTION				CURRENT SUBSCRIPTIONS			
Lib	Print	Micro	Audio	Total	Print	Micro	Audio	Total
ASU	8,221	1,500	0	9,721	6,500	0	0	6,500
CIT	U	0	0	U	3,989	0	0	3,989
MSU	0	0	0	0	8,260	0	0	8,260
NWU	7,400	16	0	7,416	U	11	0	11
SIU	15,946	U	0	15,946	5,172	45	0	5,217
SUN	7,000	U	U	7,000	2,640	U	U	2,640
UAL/E	0	0	0	0	0	0	0	0
UAL/S	0	0	0	0	1,100	0	0	1,100
UAB	0	0	0	0	5,000	4	0	5,004
UAR	8,000	0	0	8,000	4,284	0	0	4,284
UCR	3,762	20	10	3,792	1,587	2	1	1,590
UCS	4,456	U	0	4,456	2,307	U	0	2,307
UGL	13,200	U	0	13,200	7,260	87	0	7,347
UKL	12,264	27	0	12,291	6,186	25	0	6,211
UMA/E	U	U	U	1,807	U	U	U	614
UMA/S	U	U	U	3,443	U	U	U	1,424
UMN	U	U	U	U	4,266	U	U	4,266
USC	6,764	306	0	7,070	4,687	55	0	4,742
UVA	U	0	0	U	2,380	0	0	2,380
WSU	18,073	1,500	U	19,573	8,650	478	U	9,128
WAY	0	0	0	6,280	3,363	0	0	3,363
YAL	U	0	0	U	6,816	0	0	6,816
YOR	2,530	0	0	2,530	2,250	0	0	2,250

U Not reported

TABLE 6.
EXPENDITURES
(Rounded to nearest US dollar)

Lib	ACQUISITIONS			
	Monographs	Serials	Audiovisuals	Total
ASU	3,539,424	U	0	3,539,424
CIT	76,200	633,800	0	710,000
MSU	383,060	823,222	0	1,206,282
NWU	55,335	549,284	0	604,619
SIU	111,400	648,960	0	760,360
SUN	68,417	429,463	U	497,880
UAL/E	U	U	U	U
UAL/S	U	U	U	U
UAB	225,540	690,957	0	916,497
UAR	U	U	U	U
UCR	94,500	269,000	0	363,500
UCS	166,046	347,313	0	513,359
UGL	247,438	811,485	0	1,058,923
UKL	250,000	596,424	0	846,424
UMA/E	36,424	77,227	0	113,651
UMA/S	42,782	294,536	U	337,318
UMN	168,863	462,557	72,700	704,120
USC	164,339	535,000	0	699,339
UVA	197,512	539,960	0	737,472
WSU	197,345	890,000	0	1,087,345
WAY	141,000	532,000	0	673,000
YAL	120,200	570,255	0	690,455
YOR	113,250	370,500	0	483,750

Lib	BINDING	SALARIES	STAFF DEV	UTILITIES	OTHER
ASU	210,000	581,413	1,719	51,043	51,345
CIT	39,900	300,000	U	12,144	1,130
MSU	U	U	U	U	U
NWU	25,940	230,912	U	5,427	62,743
SIU	64,600	178,642	U	U	U
SUN	19,969	219,630	1,277	8,036	4,233
UAL/E	U	73,178	U	U	U
UAL/S	14,000	53,296	U	U	U
UAB	32,845	550,816	2,137	6,337	7,030
UAR	U	U	U	U	U
UCR	20,138	133,011	U	U	6,000
UCS	52,857	270,574	1,467	U	25,803
UGL	67,916	603,715	5,778	0	0
UKL	47,635	335,417	U	U	U
UMA/E	2,113	74,801	U	U	U
UMA/S	15,043	172,108	U	U	U
UMN	58,400	537,023	U	3,500	47,618
USC	24,455	170,106	17,238	45,000	6,475
UVA	U	336,049	1,100	12,729	U
WSU	65,064	623,546	5,567	U	U
WAY	29,500	289,000	U	U	U
YAL	56,595	556,890	U	20,000	20,000
YOR	U	114,705	U	2,250	26,000

U Not reported

TABLE 7.
EXPENDITURES BY SUBJECT
(Rounded to nearest US dollar)

Lib	MATHEMATICS				COMPUTER SCIENCE			
	Mono-Graphs	Serials	Audio	Total	Mono-Graphs	Serials	Audio	Total
ASU	U	U	U	U	U	U	U	U
CIT	2,500	53,500	0	56,000	5,000	10,000	0	15,000
MSU	18,800	63,491	0	82,291	U	0	0	U
NWU	U	U	U	U	U	U	U	U
SIU	U	U	U	U	U	U	U	U
SUN	6,272	49,048	U	55,320	4,026	10,673	0	14,699
UAL/E	0	0	0	0	0	0	0	0
UAL/S	U	U	U	U	U	U	U	U
UAB	U	U	U	U	U	U	U	U
UAR	U	U	U	U	4,600	U	U	4,600
UCR	U	U	U	U	U	U	U	U
UCS	U	U	U	U	U	U	U	U
UGL	17,333	U	0	17,333	U	U	U	U
UKL	U	U	U	U	U	U	U	U
UMA/E	0	0	0	0	0	0	0	0
UMA/S	6,020	3,990	200	10,210	6,995	1,807	0	8,802
UMN	11,174	42,739	3,102	57,015	0	0	0	0
USC	27,452	89,345	0	116,797	8,888	29,425	0	38,313
UVA	7,554	47,601	0	55,155	0	0	0	0
WSU	8,875	62,139	0	71,014	7,680	18,773	0	26,453
WAY	14,000	47,900	0	61,900	14,300	19,800	0	34,100
YAL	7,000	42,000	0	49,000	0	0	0	0
YOR	13,350	42,937	0	56,287	20,737	9,862	0	30,599

Lib	ASTRONOMY				PHYSICS			
	Mono-Graphs	Serials	Audio	Total	Mono-Graphs	Serials	Audio	Total
ASU	U	U	U	U	U	U	U	U
CIT	9,300	31,500	0	40,800	8,000	69,000	0	77,000
MSU	0	0	0	0	9,500	83,815	0	93,315
NWU	U	U	U	U	U	U	U	U
SIU	U	U	U	U	U	U	U	U
SUN	0	0	0	0	6,875	57,068	0	63,943
UAL/E	0	0	0	0	0	0	0	0
UAL/S	U	U	U	U	U	U	U	U
UAB	0	0	0	0	U	U	U	U
UAR	0	0	0	0	0	0	0	0
UCR	U	U	U	U	U	U	U	U
UCS	U	U	U	U	U	U	U	U
UGL	2,244	U	U	2,244	13,576	U	U	13,576
UKL	U	U	U	U	U	U	U	U
UMA/E	0	0	0	0	0	0	0	0
UMA/S	100	361	0	461	5,308	6,812	0	12,120
UMN	0	0	0	0	10,997	62,140	6,205	79,342
USC	4,594	14,445	0	19,039	20,011	65,270	0	85,281
UVA	4,342	11,872	0	16,214	16,227	78,722	0	94,949
WSU	0	0	0	0	0	0	0	0
WAY	U	U	U	U	16,100	73,600	0	89,700
YAL	0	0	0	0	0	0	0	0
YOR	0	0	0	0	10,125	89,437	0	99,562

U Not reported

TABLE 7 (continued)

Lib	CHEMISTRY				EARTH SCIENCES			
	Mono-Graphs	Serials	Audio	Total	Mono-Graphs	Serials	Audio	Total
ASU	U	U	U	U	U	U	U	U
CIT	10,800	124,400	0	135,200	14000	55,800	0	69,800
MSU	16,200	116,705	0	132,905	U	0	0	U
NWU	U	U	U	U	U	U	U	U
SIU	U	U	U	U	U	U	U	U
SUN	9,289	116,246	0	125,535	1,785	14,956	0	16,741
UAL/E	0	0	0	0	0	0	0	0
UAL/S	U	U	U	U	U	U	U	U
UAB	U	U	U	U	U	U	U	U
UAR	U	U	U	U	U	U	U	U
UCR	U	U	U	U	U	U	U	U
UCS	U	U	U	U	0	0	0	0
UGL	19,540	U	U	19,540	28330	U	U	28,330
UKL	U	U	U	U	U	U	U	U
UMA/E	0	0	0	0	0	0	0	0
UMA/S	2,920	6,439	200	9,559	5,590	2,718	0	8,308
UMN	28,660	132,272	10,198	171,130	15013	32,959	11,933	59,905
USC	21,091	69,550	0	90,641	15000	48,150	0	63,150
UVA	9,303	102,765	0	112,068	14832	55,281	0	70,113
WSU	33,081	226,853	0	259,934	0	0	0	0
WAY	17,100	123,300	0	140,400	3,100	21,700	0	24,800
YAL	3,000	56,000	0	59,000	10000	44,500	0	54,500
YOR	13,800	67,875	0	81,675	5,775	675	0	6,450

Lib	BIOLOGICAL SCIENCES				ENGINEERING			
	Mono-Graphs	Serials	Audio	Total	Mono-Graphs	Serials	Audio	Total
ASU	U	U	U	U	U	U	U	U
CIT	7,000	137,800	0	144,800	19,600	151800	0	171,400
MSU	U	0	0	U	30,600	100805	0	131,405
NWU	U	U	U	U	U	U	U	U
SIU	U	U	U	U	15,000	5,000	0	20,000
SUN	4,250	51,920	0	56,170	13,042	67,134	0	80,176
UAL/E	0	0	0	0	U	0	0	U
UAL/S	U	U	U	U	U	U	U	U
UAB	U	U	U	U	U	U	U	U
UAR	16,590	U	U	16,590	23,040	U	U	23,040
UCR	U	U	U	U	U	U	U	U
UCS	0	0	0	0	U	U	U	U
UGL	41,228	U	U	41,228	24,260	U	U	24,260
UKL	U	U	U	U	U	U	U	U
UMA/E	0	0	0	0	54,791	104835	0	159,626
UMA/S	31,000	7,621	200	38,821	0	0	0	0
UMN	0	0	0	0	78,910	183956	22107	284,973
USC	27,303	88,810	0	116113	40,000	130005	0	170,005
UVA	8,860	56,902	0	65,762	47,585	92,586	0	140,171
WSU	21,056	117642	0	138698	32,071	125270	0	157,341
WAY	28,400	149200	0	177600	34,900	85,500	0	120,400
YAL	0	0	0	0	20,000	80,000	0	100,000
YOR	31,050	90,450	0	121500	0	0	0	0

U Not reported

TABLE 7 (continued)

	AGRICULTURE				MEDICINE			
Lib	Mono-Graphs	Serials	Audio	Total	Mono-Graphs	Serials	Audio	Total
ASU	0	0	0	0	0	0	0	0
CIT	0	0	0	0	0	0	0	0
MSU	0	0	0	0	0	0	0	0
NWU	0	0	0	0	0	0	0	0
SIU	U	U	U	U	10,000	23,800	0	33,800
SUN	0	0	0	0	0	0	0	0
UAL/E	0	0	0	0	0	0	0	0
UAL/S	0	0	0	0	0	0	0	0
UAB	U	U	U	U	0	0	0	0
UAR	11,050	U	U	11,050	5,530	U	U	5,530
UCR	0	0	0	0	0	0	0	0
UCS	0	0	0	0	0	0	0	0
UGL	10,591	U	U	10,591	63,137	U	U	63,137
UKL	0	0	0	0	0	0	0	0
UMA/E	0	0	0	0	0	0	0	0
UMA/S	0	0	0	0	100	383	0	483
UMN	0	0	0	0	0	0	0	0
USC	0	0	0	0	0	0	0	0
UVA	0	0	0	0	0	0	0	0
WSU	27,393	76,164	0	103557	11,361	27,699	0	39,060
WAY	0	0	0	0	0	0	0	0
YAL	0	0	0	0	0	0	0	0
YOR	0	0	0	0	0	0	0	0

	NURSING				VETERINARY MEDICINE			
Lib	Mono-Graphs	Serials	Audio	Total	Mono-Graphs	Serials	Audio	Total
ASU	0	0	0	0	0	0	0	0
CIT	0	0	0	0	0	0	0	0
MSU	U	0	0	U	U	0	0	U
NWU	0	0	0	0	0	0	0	0
SIU	0	0	0	0	0	0	0	0
SUN	0	0	0	0	0	0	0	0
UAL/E	0	0	0	0	0	0	0	0
UAL/S	0	0	0	0	0	0	0	0
UAB	0	0	0	0	0	0	0	0
UAR	U	U	U	U	U	U	U	U
UCR	0	0	0	0	0	0	0	0
UCS	0	0	0	0	0	0	0	0
UGL	0	0	0	0	3,864	U	U	3,864
UKL	0	0	0	0	0	0	0	0
UMA/E	0	0	0	0	0	0	0	0
UMA/S	0	0	0	0	0	0	0	0
UMN	0	0	0	0	0	0	0	0
USC	0	0	0	0	0	0	0	0
UVA	0	0	0	0	0	0	0	0
WSU	0	0	0	0	29,059	131,360	0	160,419
WAY	8,600	5,300	0	13,900	0	0	0	0
YAL	0	0	0	0	0	0	0	0
YOR	0	0	0	0	0	0	0	0

U Not reported

TABLE 7 (continued)

	HOME ECONOMICS				OTHER (Totals)			
Lib	Mono-Graphs	Serials	Audio	Total	Mono-Graphs	Serials	Audio	Total
ASU	0	0	0	0	0	0	0	0
CIT	0	0	0	0	0	0	0	0
MSU	U	0	0	U	307,960	585,306	0	893,266
NWU	0	0	0	0	0	0	0	0
SIU	U	U	U	U	U	U	U	U
SUN	0	0	0	0	0	0	0	0
UAL/E	0	0	0	0	0	0	0	0
UAL/S	0	0	0	0	0	0	0	0
UAB	U	U	U	U	U	U	U	U
UAR	U	U	U	U	31,300	U	U	31,300
UCR	0	0	0	0	0	0	0	0
UCS	0	0	0	0	U	U	U	U
UGL	3,250	U	U	3,250	29,556	107,832	U	137,388
UKL	0	0	0	0	U	U	U	U
UMA/E	0	0	0	0	0	0	0	0
UMA/S	0	0	0	0	4,480	728	0	5,208
UMN	0	0	0	0	22,781	8,481	4,854	36,116
USC	0	0	0	0	0	0	0	0
UVA	0	0	0	0	88,810	94,231	0	183,041
WSU	0	0	0	0	36,649	122,171	0	158,820
WAY	4,500	5,700	0	10,200	0	0	0	0
YAL	0	0	0	0	57,500	331,655	0	389,155
YOR	0	0	0	0	18,450	68,925	0	87,375

U Not reported

TABLE 8.
PERSONNEL

Library	PROFESSIONAL			
	Adm	PS	TS	Total
Arizona State University	1.00	8.00	0.00	9.00
Cal Inst of Technology	0.00	6.00	0.00	6.00
Michigan State University	2.00	10.80	0.00	12.80
Northwestern University	0.00	3.10	0.90	4.00
S Ill Univ @ Carbondale	0.00	4.00	0.00	4.00
SUNY - Buffalo	1.00	6.00	0.00	7.00
Univ of Alabama/Eng	U	U	U	U
Univ of Alabama/Science	0.00	1.00	1.00	2.00
University of Alberta	1.00	6.00	0.00	7.00
University of Arizona	1.00	6.50	0.00	7.50
Univ of Cal @ Riverside	0.50	1.50	0.00	2.00
Univ of Cal @ San Diego	1.00	2.50	0.50	4.00
Univ of Georgia Libraries	2.00	9.00	4.00	15.00
University of Kansas	1.00	4.00	0.00	5.00
Univ of Manitoba/Eng	U	U	U	U
Univ of Manitoba/Science	U	U	U	2.00
University of Minnesota	1.00	9.00	0.00	10.00
Univ of Southern Cal	1.00	2.00	0.00	3.00
University of Virginia	1.00	1.00	2.00	4.00
Wash State University	0.75	7.43	0.31	8.49
Wayne State University	0.00	4.50	0.00	4.50
Yale University	1.00	5.00	1.00	7.00
York University	0.00	4.00	0.00	4.00

Lib	SUPPORT				HOURLY				GRAND TOTAL FTE
	Adm	PS	TS	Total	Adm	PS	TS	Total	
ASU	1.00	26.00	0.00	27.00	0.00	10.00	0.00	10.00	46.00
CIT	0.00	2.00	5.00	7.00	0.00	0.00	2.00	2.00	15.00
MSU	0.00	9.00	5.00	14.00	0.00	0.00	0.00	0.00	26.80
NWU	0.00	4.00	2.20	6.20	0.00	9.00	2.00	11.00	21.20
SIU	0.00	1.00	0.00	1.00	0.00	3.80	0.00	3.80	8.80
SUN	2.00	2.50	0.00	4.50	0.00	0.00	0.00	0.00	11.50
UAL/E	U	U	U	U	U	U	U	U	U
UAL/S	0.00	2.00	0.00	2.00	0.00	2.00	0.00	2.00	6.00
UAB	2.00	9.00	8.00	19.00	0.00	15.00	0.00	15.00	41.00
UAR	1.00	3.50	2.00	6.50	0.00	2.50	2.00	4.50	18.50
UCR	0.50	1.50	3.00	5.00	0.00	0.00	0.00	0.00	7.00
UCS	1.00	4.50	3.50	9.00	0.00	3.00	1.00	4.00	17.00
UGL	1.00	13.50	11.50	26.00	0.00	8.00	4.20	12.20	53.20
UKL	0.50	4.00	4.50	9.00	0.00	9.00	2.00	11.00	25.00
UMA/E	U	U	U	U	U	U	U	U	U
UMA/S	U	U	U	8.00	U	U	U	1.09	11.09
UMN	2.00	11.00	1.00	14.00	0.30	15.00	0.00	15.30	39.30
USC	0.00	6.00	0.00	6.00	0.00	5.50	0.00	5.50	14.50
UVA	1.00	10.50	4.00	15.50	0.00	4.00	1.00	5.00	24.50
WSU	0.25	9.29	11.06	20.60	0.00	10.14	4.89	15.03	44.12
WAY	1.00	5.00	2.00	8.00	0.00	4.00	1.00	5.00	17.50
YAL	0.00	9.00	7.00	16.00	0.00	7.00	2.00	9.00	32.00
YOR	0.00	0.00	0.00	0.00	0.00	8.00	0.00	8.00	12.00

U Not reported

TABLE 9.
BUILDING USE AND ACCESS HOURS

Library	ATTENDANCE	HOURS OPEN	REFERENCE HOURS	
			One Prof	Total
ASU	1,051,974	105.00	91.00	232.00
CIT	U	126.00	48.00	240.00
MSU	U	113.00	75.00	383.00
NWU	322,098	170.25	42.50	U
SIU	U	92.25	71.00	71.00
SUN	1,108,286	100.75	65.00	65.00
UAL/E	106,747	109.00	30.00	30.00
UAL/S	U	101.00	45.00	90.00
UAB	1,311,467	174.00	66.50	113.50
UAR	845,539	118.00	83.00	101.00
UCR	90,297	83.00	40.00	78.00
UCS	253,835	99.00	40.00	45.00
UGL	648,000	100.50	79.00	123.00
UKL	391,410	138.00	30.00	72.00
UMA/E	265,360	70.50	35.00	35.00
UMA/S	440,970	78.50	56.00	56.00
UMN	U	122.00	53.00	78.00
USC	443,878	90.00	52.00	69.00
UVA	368,743	94.00	46.00	U
WSU	688,578	112.00	68.00	68.00
WAY	441,810	85.00	66.00	66.00
YAL	U	102.00	42.50	42.50
YOR	U	80.00	46.00	46.00

U Not reported

TABLE 10.
CIRCULATION PERIODS

| | UNBOUND JNLS | | | | BOUND JNLS | | | | MONOGRAPHS | | | |
| | FACULTY | | STUDENTS | | FACULTY | | STUDENTS | | FACULTY | | STUDENTS | |
Lib	Nml	Ren	Nml	Ren	Nml	Ren	Nml	Ren	Nml	Ren	Nml	Ren
ASU	U	U	U	U	U	U	U	U	150	150	90+ 14*	90+ 14*
CIT	ON	–	ON	–	ON	–	ON	–	28	28	28	28
MSU	N	–	N	–	N	–	N	–	70	0	14	14
NWU	N	–	N	–	N	–	N	–	28	28	28	28
SIU	5	5	.25+ ON*	0	5	5	.25+ ON*	0	112	112	56+ 28*	56+ 28*
SUN	N	–	N	–	N	–	N	–	28	28	28	28
UAL/E	N	–	N	–	5	0	N	–	90	90	21	21
UAL/S	N	–	N	–	5	5	5	5	90	90	30	30
UAB	3	0	3	0	3	0	3	0	180	180	14	14
UAR	N	–	N	–	N	–	N	–	180	180	90+ 21*	90+ 21*
UCR	U	U	U	U	U	U	U	U	U	U	U	U
UCS	1	–	1	–	1	1	1	1	90	90	28	28
UGL	N	–	N	–	3	3	ON	–	365	–	28	28
UKL	1	1	1	1	1	1	1	1	120	120	28	28
UMA/E	1	0	1	0	1	0	1	0	7/60	7/60	7/60	7/60
UMA/S	1	0	1	0	7/1	7/0	7/1	7/0	7/60	1/NL	7/60	NL
UMN	1	1	1	1	1	1	1	1	365	–	70+ 30*	70+ 30*
USC	0	0	0	0	0	0	0	0	90	90	28	28
UVA	ON	0	ON	0	7	0	7	0	150	NL	30	NL
WSU	N	–	N	–	.08	.08	.08	.08	30	SM	30	30
WAY	N	–	N	–	N	–	N	–	91	91	28	28
YAL	N	–	N	–	N	–	N	–	14	5	14	5
YOR	0	0	0	0	0	0	0	0	100	100	14	14

*	Undergraduates	ON	Overnight
+	Graduates	NL	No limit
SM	Semester	U	Not reported

TABLE 10 (continued)

	GOVT DOCUMENTS				MICROFORMS				AUDIOVISUALS			
	FACULTY		STUDENTS		FACULTY		STUDENTS		FACULTY		STUDENTS	
Lib	Nml	Ren	Nml	Ren	Nml	Ren	Nml	Ren	Nml	Ren	Nml	Ren
ASU	U	U	U	U	150	150	90+ 14*	90+ 14*	3	3	3	3
CIT	14	14	14	14	N	-	N	-	N	-	N	-
MSU	70	0	14	14	N	-	N	-	N	-	N	-
NWU	28	28	28	28	N	-	N	-	N	-	N	-
SIU	112	112	56+ 28*	56+ 28*	14	14	14	14	N	-	N	-
SUN	28	28	28	28	28	28	28	28	N	-	N	-
UAL/E	90	90	21	21	N	-	N	-	N	-	N	-
UAL/S	-	-	-	-	N	-	N	-	N	-	N	-
UAB	14	14	14	14	3	0	3	0	-	-	-	-
UAR	U	U	U	U	U	U	U	U	U	U	U	U
UCR	U	U	U	U	U	U	U	U	U	U	U	U
UCS	-	-	-	-	28	-	7	-	-	-	-	-
UGL	365	-	28	28	N	-	N	-	N	-	N	-
UKL	120	120	28	28	120	120	28	28	-	-	-	-
UMA/E	7	7	7	7	7/60	7/60	7/60	7/60	-	-	-	-
UMA/S	7	NL	7	NL	1	0	1	0	-	-	-	-
UMN	7	7	7	7	7	7	7	7	7	7	7	7
USC	90	90	28	28	.25	0	.25	0	-	-	-	-
UVA	NL	-	NL	-	N	-	N	-	-	-	-	-
WSU	30	SM	30	30	30	SM	30	30	-	-	-	-
WAY	91	91	28	28	N	-	N	-	-	-	-	-
YAL	14	5	14	5	N	-	N	-	7	7	7	7
YOR	100	100	14	14	-	-	-	-	-	-	-	-

```
*    Undergraduates
+    Graduates
NL   No limit
SM   Semester
U    Not reported
```

TABLE 11.
COLLECTION USE AND INTERLIBRARY LOAN

Library	CIRCULATION			
	External	Closed Res	In-house	Photo
ASU	108,662	28,504	61,616	U
CIT	40,000	4,300	0	700,000
MSU	U	U	U	U
NWU	23,890	14,131	86,824	1,203,000
SIU	U	U	U	U
SUN	32,959	12,794	76,489	663,163
UAL/E	9,874	8,618	0	163,311
UAL/S	13,000	1,400	0	U
UAB	154,333	0	0	U
UAR	143,293	61,112	1,411,784	934,238
UCR	34,531	U	34,633	U
UCS	46,299	22,094	59,781	468,253
UGL	90,000	14,000	U	1,564,163
UKL	95,985	U	69,344	U
UMA/E	56,295	0	32,013	U
UMA/S	89,283	35,218	87,940	U
UMN	186,492	U	U	U
USC	42,620	17,500	159,250	421,260
UVA	46,011	38,600	0	U
WSU	117,236	U	199,631	1,401,227
WAY	36,656	8,591	101,088	275,243
YAL	38,422	U	U	1,640,000
YOR	54,000	U	137,000	724,000

Library	INTERLIBRARY LOAN		
	Items Borrowed	Requests Received	Requests Filled
Arizona State University	4,816	20,584	12,455
California Inst of Technology	2,827	6,000	5,649
Michigan State University	4,049	U	6,299
Northwestern University	1,814	U	1,365
S Ill Univ @ Carbondale	1,690	U	U
SUNY - Buffalo	2,110	1,220	676
University of Alabama/Eng	114	563	228
University of Alabama/Science	150	900	900
University of Alberta	3,909	5,060	U
University of Arizona	1,032	U	U
Univ of California @ Riverside	U	U	858
Univ of California @ San Diego	535	U	1,649
University of Georgia Libraries	U	U	U
University of Kansas	2,289	U	U
University of Manitoba/Eng	465	197	175
University of Manitoba/Science	450	600	560
University of Minnesota	U	U	U
University of Southern Cal	U	U	U
University of Virginia	2,203	452	975
Washington State University	1,479	8,364	5,153
Wayne State University	751	3,132	549
Yale University	459	1,536	1,051
York University	540	460	U

U Not reported

TABLE 12.
INFORMATION SERVICES AND LIBRARY INSTRUCTION

| | TRANSACTIONS | | | LIBRARY INSTRUCTION | | | | | |
| | | | | TOURS | | LECTURES | | COURSES | |
Lib	Direct	Ref	Total	Ses	Stud	Ses	Stud	Ses	Stud
ASU	17,226	62,468	79,694	21	143	41	798	1	10
CIT	U	U	U	0	0	0	0	0	0
MSU	U	U	U	0	0	0	0	0	0
NWU	U	2,040	2,040	6	18	3	21	0	0
SIU	U	U	U	0	0	10	230	1	8
SUN	62,036	9,152	71,188	40	488	6	120	28	700
UAL/E	U	U	U	0	0	12	258	0	0
UAL/S	U	U	U	4	80	0	0	0	0
UAB	4,663	31,298	35,961	58	1,110	0	0	0	0
UAR	12,232	39,648	51,880	0	0	62	1,294	0	0
UCR	438	3,718	4,156	U	U	9	U	0	0
UCS	U	10,044	10,044	11	206	7	206	0	0
UGL	U	U	U	15	41	26	422	0	0
UKL	1,657	4,663	6,320	3	60	10	150	0	0
UMA/E	U	2,795	2,795	21	550	0	0	0	0
UMA/S	U	8,002	8,002	32	717	0	0	0	0
UMN	U	U	U	U	U	U	U	1	20
USC	75,000	6,250	81,250	50	750	0	0	0	0
UVA	U	U	U	20	315	4	34	0	0
WSU	U	U	U	14	168	159	1,441	0	0
WAY	24,000	17,424	41,424	24	432	0	0	0	0
YAL	U	U	U	U	U	0	0	0	0
YOR	U	U	U	16	70	2	25	0	0

U   Not reported

TABLE 13.
DATABASE ACCESSES

Lib	AGR	BIO	CA	COMP	CP	EI	INS	MAT	MED	NTIS	SCI	OTH	Total
ASU	15	70	343	99	4	4	81	3	381	102	33	2256	3,391
CIT	U	U	U	U	U	U	U	U	U	U	U	U	2,099
MSU	35	251	52	13	0	0	13	6	551	1	15	225	1,162
NWU	0	13	51	24	0	0	10	2	15	11	3	27	156
SIU	68	53	59	9	0	0	4	0	325	18	2	48	586
SUN	0	58	75	61	0	1	39	14	0	84	24	156	512
UAL/E	U	U	U	U	U	U	U	U	U	U	U	U	U
UAL/S	U	U	U	U	U	U	U	U	U	U	U	U	U
UAB	U	U	U	U	U	U	U	U	U	U	U	U	341
UAR	U	U	U	U	U	U	U	U	U	U	U	U	462
UCR	U	U	U	U	U	U	U	U	U	U	U	U	70
UCS	0	0	60	8	0	0	46	17	0	3	12	19	165
UGL	167	107	182	16	2	0	4	2	546	54	15	474	1,569
UKL	0	30	20	4	0	4	2	0	77	2	1	24	164
UMA/E	3	0	0	74	0	12	18	1	3	59	4	141	315
UMA/S	0	0	0	0	0	0	0	0	1	0	0	3	4
UMN	1	4	61	90	1	28	51	2	8	25	17	73	361
USC	0	133	129	44	1	2	133	3	140	51	81	357	1,074
UVA	U	U	U	U	U	U	U	U	U	U	U	U	277
WSU	370	405	214	26	0	1	42	1	910	58	78	806	2,911
WAY	5	35	15	21	0	0	25	0	29	5	7	34	176
YAL	U	35	62	U	0	0	16	U	61	U	0	51	225
YOR	U	U	U	U	U	U	U	U	U	U	U	U	248

U Not reported

TABLE 14.
TYPES OF SEARCHES

Library	END-USER	SDI	REFERENCE			
			Short	How Many	LC/ Free	How Many
Arizona State University	0	2	yes	U	yes	1,084
Cal Inst of Technology	0	5	yes	U	yes	U
Michigan State University	0	4	yes	U	yes	2,372
Northwestern University	317	10	no	-	yes	17
S Ill Univ @ Carbondale	0	2	yes	36	no	-
SUNY - Buffalo	0	0	no	-	no	-
Univ of Alabama/Eng	167	0	no	-	no	-
Univ of Alabama/Science	0	0	no	-	no	-
University of Alberta	0	0	yes	141	yes	38
University of Arizona	986	0	yes	U	yes	395
Univ of Cal @ Riverside	U	0	yes	U	yes	U
Univ of Cal @ San Diego	0	1	yes	U	yes	185
Univ of Georgia Libraries	0	46	yes	U	yes	114
University of Kansas	0	0	no	-	no	-
Univ of Manitoba/Eng	0	0	no	-	no	-
Univ of Manitoba/Science	0	0	no	-	no	-
University of Minnesota	0	1	yes	U	no	-
Univ of Southern California	0	0	no	-	no	-
University of Virginia	0	0	no	-	no	-
Washington State University	0	29	yes	56	yes	430
Wayne State University	0	0	no	-	no	-
Yale University	0	0	no	-	no	-
York University	0	7	no	-	no	-

U Not reported

TABLE 15.
FEES FOR SERVICE

Library	SELF-SERVICE PHOTOCOPYING			MEDIATED PHOTOCOPYING		
	Stud	Fac	Non	Stud	Fac	Non
ASU	0.10	0.10	0.10	U	U	U
CIT	0.10	0.10	0.10	1.20	1.20	2.00
MSU	0.05	0.05	0.05	1.50	1.50	1.50
NWU	0.08	0.08	0.08	n	n	n
SIU	0.10	0.10	0.10	2.00	2.00	2.00
SUN	0.05	0.05	0.05	5.00	5.00	3.75
UAL/E	0.05	0.05	0.05	U	U	U
UAL/S	0.05	0.05	0.05	n	n	n
UAB	0.10	0.10	0.10	1.50	1.50	1.50
UAR	0.10	0.10	0.10	1.00	1.00	1.00
UCR	0.05	0.00	0.00	n	0.00	0.00
UCS	0.10	0.07	0.10	3.50	3.50	6.00
UGL	0.05	0.05	0.05	n	n	n
UKL	0.05	0.05	0.05	n	n	n
UMA/E	0.05	0.05	0.05	n	n	n
UMA/S	0.05	0.05	0.05	n	n	n
UMN	0.10	0.10	0.10	0.80	0.80	0.80
USC	0.10	0.10	0.10	n	n	n
UVA	0.05	0.05	0.05	U	U	U
WSU	0.05	0.05	0.05	1.00	1.00	1.00
WAY	0.10	0.05	0.10	3.00	3.00	5.00
YAL	0.05	0.05	0.05	1.00	1.00	1.00
YOR	0.05	0.05	0.05	n	n	n

Library	REFERENCE/ RESEARCH			DATABASE SEARCHING		
	Stud	Fac	Non	Stud	Fac	Non
ASU	U	U	U	V	V	V
CIT	n	n	30	V	V	V
MSU	U	U	U	V	V	V
NWU	n	n	n	V	V	V
SIU	n	n	n	V	V	V
SUN	0	0	30	V	V	V
UAL/E	U	U	U	n	n	n
UAL/S	n	n	n	V	V	V
UAB	n	n	n	V	V	V
UAR	0	0	0	V	V	V
UCR	n	n	n	0	0	0
UCS	0	0	0	0	0	n
UGL	n	n	n	V	V	V
UKL	0	0	0	V	V	V
UMA/E	0	0	30	V	V	V
UMA/S	0	0	0	V	V	V
UMN	0	0	0	V	V	V
USC	n	n	n	5	0	n
UVA	U	U	U	U	U	U
WSU	0	0	0	V	V	V
WAY	0	0	0	V	V	V
YAL	0	0	30	0	0	30
YOR	n	n	n	V	V	30

U Not reported

TABLE 15 (continued)

Lib	VENDOR			LABOR			OVERHEAD			DIST	SHORT SCH
	Stud	Fac	Non	Stud	Fac	Non	Stud	Fac	Non		
ASU	yes	yes	yes	no	no	no	no	no	yes	no	0
CIT	yes	yes	yes	no	no	yes	yes	yes	yes	no	0
MSU	yes	yes	yes	no	no	no	yes	yes	yes	no	0
NWU	yes	yes	yes	no	no	no	yes	yes	yes	no	0
SIU	yes	yes	yes	no	no	yes	no	no	no	yes	-
SUN	yes	yes	yes	no	no	yes	no	no	yes	no	-
UAL/E	U	U	U	U	U	U	U	U	U	no	-
UAL/S	yes	yes	yes	no	no	no	no	no	no	no	-
UAB	yes	yes	yes	no	no	no	no	no	yes	no	0
UAR	U	U	U	U	U	U	U	U	U	no	0
UCR	no	no	no	no	no	no	no	no	no	yes	0
UCS	no	no	no	yes	yes	no	yes	yes	no	no	0
UGL	yes	yes	yes	0	0	0	0	0	0	no	0
UKL	no	no	no	yes	yes	yes	yes	yes	yes	no	-
UMA/E	yes	yes	yes	0	0	yes	0	0	0	no	-
UMA/S	yes	yes	yes	no	no	no	no	no	yes	no	-
UMN	U	U	U	U	U	U	U	U	U	no	-
USC	no	no	no	no	no	no	no	no	no	no	-
UVA	U	U	U	U	U	U	U	U	U	no	-
WSU	yes	yes	yes	0	0	yes	0	0	0	no	-
WAY	yes	yes	yes	no	no	yes	yes	yes	yes	no	0
YAL	yes	yes	yes	no	no	yes	no	no	no	no	-
YOR	yes	yes	yes	0	0	0	0	0	0	no	-

U   Not reported

TABLE 16.
PENALTY FEES - MAXIMUM OVERDUE FEES

	UNBOUND JNLS			BOUND JNLS			MONOGRAPHS		
Lib	Stud	Fac	Non	Stud	Fac	Non	Stud	Fac	Non
ASU	0.00	0.00	0.00	0.00	0.00	0.00	10.00	10.00	10.00
CIT	0.00	0.00	0.00	0.00	0.00	0.00	0.00	0.00	0.00
MSU	N	N	N	NM	0.00	NM	NM	0.00	NM
NWU	N	N	N	N	N	N	5.00	0.00	5.00
SIU	5.00	5.00	5.00	5.00	5.00	5.00	5.00	5.00	5.00
SUN	N	N	N	N	N	N	25.00	0.00	25.00
UAL/E	N	N	N	10.00	0.00	0.00	10.00	0.00	0.00
UAL/S	N	N	N	15.00	15.00	15.00	10.00	10.00	10.00
UAB	10.50	0.00	10.50	10.50	0.00	10.50	10.50	0.00	10.50
UAR	N	N	N	N	N	N	25.00	25.00	25.00
UCR	3.00	3.00	3.00	5.00	5.00	5.00	5.00	5.00	5.00
UCS	5.00	5.00	5.00	5.00	5.00	5.00	5.00	5.00	5.00
UGL	N	0.00	N	N	0.00	N	18.25	0.00	18.25
UKL	10.00	10.00	10.00	10.00	10.00	10.00	5.00	5.00	5.00
UMA/E	0.00	0.00	0.00	0.00	0.00	0.00	0.00	0.00	0.00
UMA/S	0.00	0.00	0.00	0.00	0.00	0.00	0.00	0.00	0.00
UMN	10.00	0.00	10.00	10.00	0.00	10.00	0.00	0.00	0.00
USC	N	N	N	N	N	N	20.00	0.00	20.00
UVA	10.00	0.00	10.00	10.00	0.00	10.00	6.00	0.00	6.00
WSU	N	N	N	20.00	20.00	20.00	17.50	17.50	17.50
WAY	N	N	N	N	N	N	3.00	0.00	3.00
YAL	N	N	N	N	N	N	10.00	N	10.00
YOR	0.00	0.00	0.00	0.00	0.00	0.00	15.00	15.00	15.00

	GOVT DOCUMENTS			MICROFORMS		
Library	Stud	Fac	Non	Stud	Fac	Non
ASU	0.00	0.00	0.00	10.00	10.00	10.00
CIT	0.00	0.00	0.00	0.00	0.00	0.00
MSU	NM	0.00	NM	N	N	N
NWU	5.00	0.00	5.00	N	N	N
SIU	5.00	5.00	5.00	5.00	5.00	5.00
SUN	25.00	0.00	25.00	25.00	0.00	25.00
UAL/E	10.00	0.00	0.00	N	N	N
UAL/S	10.00	10.00	10.00	10.00	10.00	10.00
UAB	10.50	0.00	10.50	10.50	0.00	10.50
UAR	25.00	25.00	25.00	0.00	0.00	0.00
UCR	5.00	5.00	5.00	3.00	3.00	3.00
UCS	N	N	N	5.00	5.00	5.00
UGL	18.25	0.00	18.25	N	N	N
UKL	5.00	5.00	5.00	10.00	10.00	10.00
UMA/E	0.00	0.00	0.00	0.00	0.00	0.00
UMA/S	0.00	0.00	0.00	0.00	0.00	0.00
UMN	0.00	0.00	0.00	0.00	0.00	0.00
USC	20.00	0.00	20.00	0.00	0.00	0.00
UVA	0.00	0.00	0.00	N	N	N
WSU	17.50	17.50	17.50	17.50	17.50	17.50
WAY	3.00	0.00	3.00	3.00	0.00	3.00
YAL	10.00	N	10.00	N	N	N
YOR	15.00	15.00	15.00	0.00	0.00	0.00

TABLE 16 (continued)

Library	AUDIOVISUALS			RESERVES		
	Stud	Fac	Non	Stud	Fac	Non
ASU	10.00	10.00	10.00	10.00	10.00	10.00
CIT	0.00	0.00	0.00	0.00	0.00	0.00
MSU	N	N	N	15.00	0.00	15.00
NWU	N	N	N	0.00	0.00	0.00
SIU	5.00	5.00	5.00	5.00	5.00	5.00
SUN	25.00	0.00	25.00	25.00	0.00	25.00
UAL/E	N	N	N	N	N	N
UAL/S	0.00	0.00	0.00	NM	NM	NM
UAB	0.00	0.00	10.50	100.00	0.00	100.00
UAR	0.00	0.00	0.00	25.00	25.00	25.00
UCR	0.00	0.00	0.00	NM	NM	NM
UCS	N	N	N	20.00	20.00	20.00
UGL	N	N	N	18.25	0.00	18.25
UKL	N	N	N	10.00	10.00	10.00
UMA/E	0.00	0.00	0.00	15.00	15.00	0.00
UMA/S	0.00	0.00	0.00	15.00	15.00	15.00
UMN	0.00	0.00	0.00	0.00	0.00	0.00
USC	0.00	0.00	0.00	20.00	0.00	20.00
UVA	0.00	0.00	0.00	15.00	0.00	15.00
WSU	17.50	17.50	17.50	20.00	20.00	20.00
WAY	0.00	0.00	0.00	0.00	0.00	0.00
YAL	N	N	N	5.00	5.00	N
YOR	0.00	0.00	0.00	15.00	15.00	15.00

TABLE 17
PENALTY FEES - PER DAY FEES

	UNBOUND JNLS			BOUND JNLS			MONOGRAPHS		
Lib	Stud	Fac	Non	Stud	Fac	Non	Stud	Fac	Non
ASU	N	N	N	N	N	N	S	S	S
CIT	0.00	0.00	0.00	0.00	0.00	0.00	0.00	0.00	0.00
MSU	N	N	N	S	0.00	S	S	0.00	S
NWU	N	N	N	N	N	N	0.10	0.00	0.10
SIU	*	*	*	*	*	*	0.15	0.15	0.15
SUN	N	N	N	N	N	N	0.25	0.00	0.25
UAL/E	N	N	N	1.00	0.00	0.00	0.25	0.00	0.00
UAL/S	N	N	N	S	S	S	S	S	S
UAB	0.50	0.00	0.50	0.50	0.00	0.50	0.50	0.00	0.50
UAR	N	N	N	N	N	N	0.25	0.25	0.25
UCR	S	S	S	S	S	S	S	S	S
UCS	S	S	S	S	S	S	S	S	S
UGL	N	0.00	N	N	0.00	N	0.10	0.00	0.10
UKL	1.60	1.60	1.60	1.60	1.60	1.60	5.00	5.00	5.00
UMA/E	0.00	0.00	0.00	0.00	0.00	0.00	0.00	0.00	0.00
UMA/S	0.00	0.00	0.00	0.00	0.00	0.00	0.00	0.00	0.00
UMN	1.00	0.00	N	1.00	0.00	N	0.50	0.00	N
USC	N	N	N	N	N	N	0.20	0.00	0.20
UVA	1.00	0.00	1.00	1.00	0.00	1.00	0.10	0.00	0.10
WSU	N	N	N	1.00	1.00	1.00	0.25	0.25	0.25
WAY	N	N	N	N	N	N	S	S	S
YAL	N	N	N	N	N	N	0.00	0.00	0.00
YOR	0.00	0.00	0.00	0.00	0.00	0.00	0.20	0.20	0.20

* 0.25 first hour; 0.15 each additional hour

	GOVT DOCUMENTS			MICROFORMS			AUDIOVISUALS		
Lib	Stud	Fac	Non	Stud	Fac	Non	Stud	Fac	Non
ASU	0.00	0.00	0.00	*	*	*	*	*	*
CIT	0.00	0.00	0.00	0.00	0.00	0.00	0.00	0.00	0.00
MSU	S	0.00	S	N	0.00	N	N	0.00	N
NWU	0.10	0.00	0.10	N	N	N	N	N	N
SIU	0.15	0.15	0.15	0.15	0.15	0.15	0.15	0.15	0.15
SUN	0.25	0.00	0.25	0.25	0.00	0.25	0.25	0.00	0.25
UAL/E	0.25	0.00	0.00	N	N	N	N	N	N
UAL/S	S	S	S	S	S	S	S	S	S
UAB	0.50	0.00	0.50	0.50	0.00	0.50	0.50	0.00	0.50
UAR	0.25	0.25	0.25	0.00	0.00	0.00	0.00	0.00	0.00
UCR	S	S	S	S	S	S	0.00	0.00	0.00
UCS	N	N	N	S	S	S	N	N	N
UGL	0.10	0.00	0.10	N	0.00	N	N	0.00	N
UKL	5.00	5.00	5.00	N	N	N	N	N	N
UMA/E	0.00	0.00	0.00	0.00	0.00	0.00	0.00	0.00	0.00
UMA/S	0.00	0.00	0.00	0.00	0.00	0.00	0.00	0.00	0.00
UMN	N	N	N	N	N	N	N	N	N
USC	0.20	0.00	0.20	0.00	0.00	0.00	0.00	0.00	0.00
UVA	0.00	0.00	0.00	N	N	N	0.00	0.00	0.00
WSU	0.25	0.25	0.25	0.25	0.25	0.25	1.00	1.00	1.00
WAY	S	S	S	N	N	N	0.00	0.00	0.00
YAL	0.00	0.00	0.00	N	N	N	0.00	0.00	N
YOR	0.20	0.20	0.20	0.00	0.00	0.00	0.00	0.00	0.00

* 1.00 first day; 0.50 each additional day; 10.00 maximum

TABLE 17 (continued)

Library	RESERVES Stud	Fac	Non	PROCESS FEE	ASSESS-MENT
ASU	**	**	**	U	av
CIT	0.00	0.00	0.00	4.00	or
MSU	S	0.00	S	15.00	av
NWU	-	0.00	0.00	15.00	or
SIU	0.25	0.25	0.25	5.00	or
SUN	8.00	0.00	N	15.00	av
UAL/E	N	N	N	5.00	av
UAL/S	8.00	8.00	8.00	5.00	or
UAB	34.00	0.00	N	10.00	av
UAR	0.00	0.00	0.00	35.00	U
UCR	S	S	S	5.00	av
UCS	13.50***	13.50	13.50	5.00	or
UGL	1.75	0.00	1.75	5.00	a/o
UKL	1.60	1.60	1.60	5.00	av
UMA/E	5.00	5.00	N	12.00	av
UMA/S	5.00	5.00	5.00	12.00	a/o
UMN	2.50	N	N	6.00	U
USC	@	0.00	@	10.00	av
UVA	8.00	0.00	8.00	5.00	or
WSU	1.00	1.00	1.00	10.00	av
WAY	0.00	0.00	0.00	10.00	av
YAL	5.00	5.00	N	15.00	or
YOR	8.00	8.00	N	15.00	av

```
**    (day)  1.00 first day; 0.50 each additional day
      (hour) 0.50 first hour; 0.25 each additional hour
***   Plus 5.00 billing fee (first day only)
@     1.00/hour S (2 hours)
      1.00/day S (1-7 days)

a/o   Average and Original
av    Average
or    Original

U     Not reported
```

TABLE 18

ACRL
SCIENCE AND TECHNOLOGY SECTION

Task Force on Comparison
of Science/Engineering Libraries

Chair

Emerson Hilker
Head, Science and Engineering Library
Wayne State University
Detroit, Michigan 48202
313-577-4373

Members

Carole Armstrong
Head, Science Libraries
Michigan State University
E. Lansing, Michigan 48824-1048
517-353-6676

A. Albert Baker
Seaver Science Library
University of Southern California
Los Angeles, California 90089-0481
213-743-0371

Lloyd A. Davidson
Seeley G. Mudd Library for Science
 and Technology
Northwestern University
Evanston, Illinois 60201

Beverlee French
Head, Science Library
University of California at San Diego
La Jolla, California 92093
619-452-3257

Alan Hagyard, Geology/Physical Science
 Resource Librarian
Geology Library
Yale University
New Haven, Connecticut 06511
203-436-2480

Robert Michaelson
Head Librarian, Science and
 Engineering Library
Northwestern University
Evanston, Illinois 60201
312-491-3057

Nestor Osorio, Science Librarian
Founders Memorial Library
Northern Illinois University
Dekalb, Illinois 60115
815-753-9837

Elizabeth Roberts
Head, Owen Science and Engineering
 Library
Washington State University
Pullman, Washington 99164-3200
509-335-2671

TABLE 19

STATISTICAL DATA FOR
ARL STAND-ALONE SCIENCE/ENGINEERING LIBRARIES
QUESTIONNAIRE

List of Participating Libraries To Date (6/30/86)

ASU	Arizona State University Daniel E. Noble Science and Engineering Library Tempe, Arizona 85287
CIT	California Institute of Technology Robert A. Milliken Memorial Library Pasadena, California 91125
MSU	Michigan State University East Lansing, Michigan 48824-1048
NWU	Northwestern University Seeley G. Mudd Library for Science and Technology Evanston, Illinois 60201
SIU	Southern Illinois University at Carbondale Science Division, Morris Library Carbondale, Illinois 62901
SUN	State University of New York (SUNY) at Buffalo Science & Engineering Library Buffalo, New York 14260
UAL/E	University of Alabama Engineering Library University, Alabama 35486
UAL/S	University of Alabama Science Library University, Alabama 35486
UAB	University of Alberta 2-10 Cameron Library Edmonton, Alberta T6C 2J8
UAR	University of Arizona Science-Engineering Library Tucson, Arizona 85721
UCR	University of California at Riverside Physical Science Library Riverside, California 92517
UCS	University of California at San Diego Science and Engineering Library La Jolla, California 92093
UGL	University of Georgia Libraries Science Library Athens, Georgia 30602

TABLE 19 (continued)

UKL	University of Kansas Lawrence, Kansas 66045
UMA/E	The University of Manitoba Engineering Library Winnipeg, Manitoba R3T 2N2
UMA/S	The University of Manitoba Science Library Winnipeg, Manitoba R3T 2N2
UMN	University of Minnesota Science and Technology Library Minneapolis, Minnesota 55455
USC	University of Southern California Seaver Science Library Los Angeles, California 90089-0481
UVA	University of Virginia Science and Engineering Library Charlottesville, Virginia 22903
WSU	Washington State University Owen Science and Engineering Library Pullman, Washington 99164-3200
WAY	Wayne State University Science and Engineering Library Detroit, Michigan 48202
YAL	Yale University Kline Science Library New Haven, Connecticut 06511
YOR	York University Steacie Science Library Downsview, Ontario M3J 1P3

SCI-TECH COLLECTIONS

Tony Stankus, Editor

This issue's collection development paper is Part II of Colette O'Connell's analysis of the literature on Computer-Aided Design and Computer-Aided Manufacturing, continuing the part that appeared in the previous issue of this journal.

In this part she provides an acronym glossary, a bibliography arranged by type of format (dictionaries, monographs, journals, etc.) and a list of associations/societies related to this topic.

CAD/CAM (Computer-Aided Design/ Computer-Aided Manufacturing): A History of the Technology and Guide to the Literature Part II

Colette O'Connell

The first section of this paper describes the development of Computer-Aided Design/Computer-Aided Manufacturing (CAD/CAM) during the last forty years. The second section consists of three appendices. APPENDIX 1 is a glossary of CAD/CAM related acronyms. Acronyms for organizations as well as terminology are included. APPENDIX 2 is a bibliography for a core CAD/CAM library collection. This bibliography was completed in May 1986, and does not include imprints published after this date. The material in this appendix is classified by format as follows: Dictionaries and Encyclopedias; Handbooks; Directories, Buyers' Guides and Evaluation Tools; Bibliographies; Abstracts and Indexes; Technical Reports; Conferences; Research and Trade Journals; Monographs; Monographic Series; Standards; Patents; and Software. APPENDIX 3 includes a directory of pertinent organizations and associations, as well as vendors providing online databases for this field.

Colette O'Connell has a BA degree in Mathematics from Rhode Island College in Providence, RI and a MLS from the State University of New York at Albany. She is the Engineering Librarian and Coordinator of Online Search Services at Folsom Library, Rensselaer Polytechnic Institute, Troy, NY 12181.

APPENDIX 1

ACRONYM GLOSSARY

ACM – Association for Computing Machinery

ACM/SIGGRAPH – Association for Computing Machinery/Special Interest Group on Computer Graphics

AMRF – Automated Manufacturing Research Facility

ANSI – American National Standards Institute

APT – Automatically Programmed Tools

AUTOPROMT – Automatic Programming of Machine Tools

CAD – Computer-Aided Design

CADAM – Computer-Aided Design and Manufacture

CADD – Computer-Aided Design and Drafting

CAD/CAM – Computer-Aided Design/Computer-Aided Manufacturing

CAE – Computer-Aided Engineering

CAM-I – Computer-Aided Manufacturing – International

CAPP – Computer-Assisted Process Planning

CARIC – Computerized Automation and Robotics Information

CASA – Computer Automated and Systems Association of the SME (Society of Manufacturing Engineers)

CIM – Computer-Integrated Manufacturing

COGO – Coordinated Geometry

CORE – Common Operational Research Equipment

CNC – Computer Numerical Control

DIN – Deutsches Institut fuer Normung (German Standards Institute)

DNC – Direct Numerical Control
FMS – Flexible Manufacturing Systems
FORTRAN – Formula Translation
GKS - Graphics Kernel Standard
GSPC – Graphics Standards Planning Committee
ICAM – Integrated Computer Aided Manufacturing
IEEE – Institute for Electrical and Electronics Engineers
IFAC – International Federation of Automatic Control
IFIP – International Federation for Information Processing
IFIP TC-5 – International Federation for Information Processing Technical Committee 5 on Computer Applications
IGES – International Graphics Exchange Specification
IPAD – Integrated Program for Aerospace-Vehicle Development
ISO – International Organization for Standardization
MAP – Manufacturing Automation Protocol
MIS – Management Information Systems
NAPLPS – North American Presentation Level Protocol Syntax
NASA – National Aeronautics and Space Administration
NASTRAN – NASA Structural Analysis
NBS – National Bureau of Standards
NC – Numerical Control
NRC/MSB – National Research Council/Manufacturing Studies Board
PHIGS – Programmer's Hierarchical Interactive Graphics Standards
SME – Society of Manufacturing Engineers
STEP – Standard for Exchange of Product Data
STRESS – Structural Engineering System Solver

APPENDIX 2

CLASSIFIED CAD/CAM BIBLIOGRAPHY

Material is listed by format as follows: Dictionaries and Encyclopedias; Handbooks; Directories, Buyer's Guide and Evaluation Tools; Bibliographies; Abstracts and Indexes; Technical Reports; Conferences; Research and Trade Journals and Newsletters; Monographs; Monographics Series; Standards; Patents; and Software. Entries which need clarification are annotated. Online databases are listed with the appropriate format and are preceded by an asterisk. A short name/address directory of database vendors is included in Appendix 3.

Dictionaries and Encyclopedias

Allan, John J., III. *The CAD/CAM Glossary*. Dallas, TX: Leading Edge Publishing, Inc., 1979.

Bindman, W. *Dictionary of Microelectronics*: *English-German, German-English*. New York: Elsevier, 1984.

Glossary of Common CAD/CAM Terms and Concepts. 4th rev. Bedford, MA: Computervision Corp., 1983.

Glossary of Computer Aided Manufacturing Terms. 3rd ed. Arlington, TX: Computer-Aided Manufacturing-International, Inc., 1982.

Hubbard, Stuart W. *The Computer Glossary*. Phoenix, AZ: The Oryx Press, 1983.

Manufacturing Engineering. Chapter 7, Facilities Design. Chapter 10, Planning and Control. Chapter 11, and Computers and Information Processing Systems. Chapter 12 in *Handbook of Industrial Engineering*, edited by Gavriel Salvendy. New York: John Wiley, 1982.

Parker, Sybil P. *McGraw-Hill Dictionary of Electronics and Computer Technology*. New York: McGraw Hill, 1984.

Represents 10,000 terms selected from *McGraw-Hill Dictionary of Scientific and Technical Terms* (3rd ed).

Preston, Edward J., George W. Crawford, and Mark E. Cotticchia. *CAD/CAM Dictionary*. New York: Marcel Dekker, 1985.

Ralston, Anthony and Reilly, Edwin D., ed. *Encyclopedia of Computer Science and Engineering*. New York: Van Nostrand Reinhold, Co., 1983.
One-volume encyclopedia.

Rosenberg, Jerry M. *Dictionary of Computers, Data Processing and Telecommunications*. New York: John Wiley, 1984.

Sobczak, Thomas V. *A Glossary of Terms for Computer-Integrated Manufacturing*. 1st ed. Dearborn, MI: Computer and Automated Systems Association of the SME, 1984.

Tver, David F. and Bolz, Roger W. *Encylopedic Dictionary of Industrial Technology: Materials, Processes and Equipment*. New York: Chapman and Hall, 1984.

Vince, John. *Dictionary of Computer Graphics*. White Plains, NY: Knowledge Industry Publications, 1984.

Handbooks

Conrac Corporation, Conrac Division. *Raster Graphics Handbook*. 2nd ed. New York: Van Nostrand Reinhold, 1985.

Drozda, Thomas J. and Wick, Charles. *Tool and Manufacturing Handbook*. 3 v. 4th ed. Dearborn, MI: Society of Manufacturing Engineers, 1983-1985.

Lightner, M.R. and Director, S.W. Computer-Aided Design of Electronic Circuits. Chapter 27 in *Electronics Engineers Handbook*, edited by Donald G. Fink and Donald Christiansen. New York: McGraw-Hill, 1982.

Machover, Carl and Blauth, Robert E. *The CAD/CAM Handbook*. Bedford, MA: Computervision Corp., 1980.

Oberg, Eric, Jones, Franklin D. and Horton, Holbrook L. *Machinery Handbook*. 22nd ed. New York: Industrial Press, Inc., 1984.

Rowbotham, George E. *Engineering and Industrial Graphics Handbook*. New York: McGraw-Hill, 1982.

Sapiro, Steve and Smith, Robert J., III. *Handbook of Design Automation*. Sunnyvale, CA: CAE Systems, Inc., 1984.

Tiecholz, Eric. *CAD/CAM Handbook*. New York: McGraw-Hill, 1985.

Directories, Buyer's Guide, and Evaluation Tools

The Contemporary Technology. Part 1, Evaluating Today's Systems. Part 2, and Survey, Review and Buyer's Guide. Part 3 in *CAD/CAM, CAE*. Cambridge MA: Daratech Associates, 1984.

Chasen, Sylvan and Dow, J.W. *The Guide for the Evaluation and Implementation of CAD/CAM Systems.* Atlanta, GA: CAD/CAM Decisions, 1980.
   Selection guide rather than a directory.

Computer Graphics Directory. San Francisco, CA: Computer Graphics World, 1984-   . Annual.

Computer Graphics Marketplace. Phoenix, AZ: Oryx Press, 1981-   . Irregular.
   Directory of manufacturers, major conferences, educational programs, publications, and organizations.

IHS Vendor Information. Englewood, Co: Information Handling Services. Current vendor catalog information.
   Online Vendor: BRS.

Interco Business Consultants, Ltd. *Computer Graphics, CAD, and CAD/CAM Product Guide and Supplier's Directory*. New York: Frost & Sullivan, Inc., 1983-   . Annual.

Flora, Philip, ed. *International CAD Directory*. Blue Ridge Summit, PA: Tab Books, 1986.

Flora, Philip, ed. *International CAM Directory*. Blue Ridge Summit, PA: Tab Books, 1986.

Marquis Who's Who Directory of Computer Graphics. Chicago, IL: Marquis Who's Who, Inc., 1984.
    Includes index by area of expertise for "Electrical CAD/CAM," "Mechanical CAD/CAM," and "Architectural and Engineering CAD/CAM."

Robotics, CAD/CAM Market Place. New York: Bowker, 1985- . Annual
    International guide to literature, research centers, consultants, manufacturers, and educational institutions for this field.

Thomas Register's Mid-year Guide to Factory Automation. New York: Thomas Publishing Co., 1986- . Semiannual.
    Includes a collection of articles from the various manufacturing trade journals, a short glossary, and a product directory.

Thomas Register of American Manufacturers and Thomas Register Catalog File. New York: Thomas Publishing Co., 1905- . Annual. Online format: *Thomas Register Online*; Online vendor: DIALOG; Includes headings, "CAD/CAM Systems," "Designers: Computer-Aided," and "Computer Graphics Services."

Bibliographies

CAD/CAM, Computer-Aided Design/Computer-Aided Manufacturing Technical Bulletin. New York: Engineering Information, Inc., 1983.
    Part of the *Technical Bulletin Series*; drawn from the *COMPENDEX* database covering January 1981 to August 1983.

CAD/CAM in the Automotive and Space Industries. Dearborn, MI: Society of Manufacturing Engineers.
    Published search from the society's *INTIME Manufacturing DataBank*.

Computer Graphics Technical Bulletin. New York: Engineering Information, Inc., 1984.

Part of the *Technical Bulletin Series*; drawn from the *COMPENDEX* database covering January 1980 to December 1983.

Havas, George D. *CAD/CAM (Computer-Aided Design/Computer-Aided Manufacturing): A Brief Guide to Materials in the Library of Congress*. Washington, DC: Science Reference Section, Science and Technology Division, Library of Congress, 1985.

LC Science Tracer Bulletin, TB 85-7.

Lee, Sharon Y. W. *Computer-Assisted Design/Computer-Assisted manufacturing: A Selected Bibliography*. Monticello, IL: Vance Bibliographies, 1983.

Public Administration Series Bibliography, P-1272.

Abstracts and Indexes

Applied Science and Technology Index. New York: H. W. Wilson, 1958- . Monthly; quarterly and annual cumulations.
   Online format: *WILSONLINE*; Online vendor: H.W. Wilson.

Business Periodicals Index. New York: H.W. Wilson, 1958- . Monthly; quarterly and annual cumulations.
   Online format: *WILSONLINE*; Online vendor: H.W. Wilson.

CAD/CAM Abstracts. New York: EIC/Intelligence Pub. Division, 1984- . Monthly.
   Online format: SUPERTECH; Online vendor: DIALOG.

Computer and Control Abstracts. London: Institution of Electrical Engineers, 1966- . Monthly; semiannual cumulations.
   Online format: *INSPEC*. Online vendor: BRS, DIALOG, SDC.

The Computer Database. Belmont, CA: Information Access Co., 1983- . Biweekly.
   Online vendor: DIALOG.

Ei Engineering Conference Index. New York: Engineering Information, Inc., 1984- . Annual.

Online format: *Ei Engineering Meetings*; Online vendor: DIALOG.

Electrical and Electronics Abstracts. London: Institution of Electrical Engineer, 1898- . Monthly; semiannual cumulations.
Online format: *INSPEC*; Online vendor: BRS, DIALOG, SDC.

Engineering Index Monthly. New York: Engineering Information, Inc., 1884- . Monthly; annual cumulations.
Online format: *COMPENDEX*; Online vendor: BRS, DIALOG, SDC.

Index to IEEE Publications. New York: Institute of Electrical and Electronics Engineers, 1973- . Annual.

INTIME Manufacturing DataBase. Dearborn, MI: Society of Manufacturing Engineers, 1973- .
Database of SME's technical papers, book, and journal articles; not commercially available; searches conducted for a fee by telephone interview.

Predicasts F&S Index United States. Cleveland, OH: Predicasts, Inc., 1960- . Quarterly; annual cumulations.
Online format: *PTS F&S Index*; Online vendor: BRS, DIALOG.

Science Citation Index. Philadelphia: Institute for Scientific Information, 1964- . Quarterly; annual cumulations.
Online service: *SCISEARCH*; Online vendor: DIALOG.

Technical Digest. Dearborn, MI: Society of Manufacturing Engineers.
Guide to all technical papers published by the Society of Manufacturing Engineers and its affiliated associations.

Technical Reports

Government Reports, Announcements and Index. Springfield, VA: National Technical Information Service, v.75, 1975- . Biweekly; annual cumulation.

Online format: *NTIS (National Technical Information Service)*; Online vendor: BRS, DIALOG, SDC.

NTIS: Manufacturing Technology: An Abstract Newsletter. Springfield, VA: National Technical Information Service, 1983- .Weekly; annual cumulation.

Current awareness abstracting tool; lists technical reports from *NTIS* database as well as published searchers from *COMPENDEX* and other databases.

Scientific and Technical Aerospace Reports. Washington, DC: U.S. National Aeronautics and Space Administration, 1963- . Semimonthly; quarterly and annual cumulations.

Online format: *Aerospace Database*; Online vendor: DIALOG.

The following organizations have published technical reports on CAD/CAM. Entries were identified by a comprehensive subject search of the *NTIS (National Technical Service)* database.

> Air Force Institute of Technology, Wright-Patterson Air Force Base, OH. School of Engineering.
>
> Army Industrial Base Engineering Activity, Rock Island, IL.
>
> Army Material Development and Readiness Command, Alexandria, VA.
>
> Bendix Corporation, Kansas City, MO.
>
> California University, Berkeley. Lawrence Berkeley Laboratory.
>
> Council for Scientific and Industrial Research, Pretoria, South Africa.
>
> Department of Energy, Washington, DC.
>
> National Aeronautics and Space Administration, Hampton, VA. Langley Research Center.
>
> Lawrence Livermore National Laboratory, CA.
>
> National Aerospace Laboratory, Amsterdam, Netherlands.
>
> Rolls Royce Ltd., Derby, England.

Sandia National Laboratories, Albuquerque, NM.

Softech; Inc., Waltham, MA.

Conferences

IEEE, IFIP, and SME sponsor most of the CAD/CAM conferences. Their conferences are listed separately below. The addresses and telephones for these organizations as well as other CAD/CAM and computer graphics groups are listed in Appendix 3. A miscellaneous category is included for other conferences in the field.

Association for Computing Machinery

ACM/SIGGRAPH Workshop on User-Oriented Design of Interactive Graphics Systems, 1976, Pittsburgh, PA. *User-Oriented Design of Interactive Graphics Systems*. New York: Association for Computing Machinery, 1977.

SIGGRAPH Conference. *Proceedings*. New York: Association for Computing Machinery, Special Interest Group on Computer Graphics, 1974-   . Annual.

Institute of Electrical and Electronics Engineers

COMPCON, 20th, 1980, San Francisco. *Tutorial and Selected Readings in Computer Graphics*. Long Beach, CA: Institute of Electrical and Electronics Engineers, 1980.

Conference on Computer Graphics, Pattern Recognition & Data Structures, 1975, Los Angeles. *Proceedings*. New York: Institute of Electrical and Electronics Engineers, 1975.

Design Automation Conference. *Proceedings*. New York: Association for Computing Machinery and the Institute for Electrical and Electronics Engineers, 1964-   . Annual.

IEEE Computer Society Conference on Computer Vision and Pattern Recognition. New York: IEEE Computer Society, 1975-   . Annual.

IEEE International Conference on Computer-Aided Design, IC-CAD. *Proceedings*. New York: Institute of Electrical and Electronics Engineers, 1984-   . Annual.

IEEE Machine Tool Industry Conference. *Proceedings*. New York: IEEE Industrial Applications Society, Machine Tools Industry Committee, 1948-   . Biennial.

International Conference and Exposition: Interactive Techniques in Computer-Aided Design, 1978, Bologna, Italy. *Proceedings*. Long Beach, CA: IEEE Computer Society, 1978.

International Conference on Pattern Recognition. *Proceedings*. New York: IEEE Computer Society, 1973-   . Biennial.

International Display Research Conference. *Proceedings*. New York: IEEE Group on Electron Devices, 1970-   . Biennial.

Workshop on Computer Vision: Representation and Control. *Proceedings*. New York: IEEE Computer Society, 1982-   . Biennial.

Workshop on Interactive Computing: CAE Electrical Engineering Education. *Proceedings*. Silver Springs, MD: IEEE Computer Society, 1982-   . Annual.

International Federation for Information Processing

IFAC/IFIP Symposium on Information Control Problems in Manufacturing Technology, 4th, 1982, Maryland. *Information Control Problems in Manufacturing Technology*. New York: Pergamon Press, 1983.

IFIP TC-5 Working Conference on Artificial Intelligence and Pattern Recognition in Computer-Aided Design, 1978, Grenoble, France. *Proceedings*. New York: North-Holland Pub. Co., 1978.

IFIP WG5.2 Working Conference on CAD Systems Framework, 1982, Riros, Norway. *CAD Systems Framework*. New York: North-Holland Pub. Co., 1978.

IFIP WG5.2 Working Conference on CAD/CAM as a Basis for the Development of Technology in Developing Nations, 1981, Sao Paulo, Brazil. *CAD/CAM as a Basis for the Development for Tech-*

nology in Developing Nations. New York: North-Holland Pub. Co., 1981.

IFIP WG5.2 Working Conference on File Structures and Data Bases for CAD, 1981, Scehein, Hesse, Germany. *File Structures and Databases for CAD*. New York: North-Holland Pub. Co., 1982.

IFIP WG5.2-5.3 Working Conference on Integration of CAD/CAM, 1983, Gaubig near Dresden. *Integration of CAD/CAM Proceedings*, New York: North-Holland Pub. Co., 1984.

IFIP WG5.2-5.3 Working Conference on Man-Machine Communications in CAD/CAM, 1980, Tokyo. *Man-Made Communications in CAD/CAM*. New York: North-Holland Pub. Co., 1981.

IFIP Working Conference on Computer-Aided Design Systems, 1976, Austin, TX. *CAD Systems*. New York: North-Holland Pub. Co., 1976.

IFIP Working Conference on Principals of Computer-Aided Design, 1972, Eindhaven, Netherlands. *Proceedings*. New York: North-Holland Pub. Co., 1973.

IFIP Workshop on Methodology in Computer Graphics, 1976, Seilac, France. *Methodology in Computer Graphics*. New York: North-Holland Pub. Co., 1977.

International IFIP Conference on Computer Applications in Production and Engineering, 1st, 1983, Amsterdam, Netherlands. *Computer Applications in Production and Engineering: Proceedings*. New York: North-Holland Pub. Co., 1984.

International IFIP/IFAC Conference on Programming Research and Operations Logistics in Advanced Manufacturing. *PROLOMAT*. New York: North-Holland Pub. Co., 1969-   . Irregular.

Society of Manufacturing Engineers

ASSEMBLEX Conference, 8th, 1982, Cleveland, OH. *Proceedings*. Dearborn, MI: Society of Manufacturing Engineers, 1982.

AUTOFACT '85, 1985, Dearborn, MI. *Proceedings*. Dearborn, MI: Society of Manufacturing Engineers, 1985.

CAD/CAM Conference, 5th, 1977, Detroit. *Proceedings*. Dearborn, MI: Society of Manufacturing Engineers, 1977.

North American Manufacturing Research Conference. *Proceedings*. (Formerly: *Manufacturing Engineering Transactions*). Dearborn, MI: Society of Manufacturing Engineers, 1972-   . Annual.

Miscellaneous

ASEE Conference, 8th, 1985, Georgia Institute of Technology. *Computer-Aided Engineering*. Washington, DC: The American Society for Engineering Education, 1985.

Automation Technology Symposium, 3rd, 1981, Monterey, CA. *Proceedings*. Englewood Cliffs, NJ: Prentice Hall, 1983.

CAD '84: International Conference and Exhibition on Computers in Design Engineering, 4th, 1980, Brighton, England. *Proceedings*. Guilford, England: IPC Science and Technology, 1980.

CAD/CAM, Robotics and Automation International Conference, 1985, Tuscon, AZ. *Proceedings*. Columbia, MO: University of Missouri, 1985.

CAM-I International Spring Seminar, 1978, Albuquerque, NM. *Proceedings*. Arlington, TX: Computer-Aided Manufacturing-International, 1978.

Computer-Aided Manufacturing-International, Inc. Meeting and Technical Conference. *Proceedings*. Arlington, TX: Computer-Aided Manufacturing-International, 1972-   . Annual.

Computer-Aided Design Conference, 1983, Anaheim, CA. *Proceedings*. New York: Morgan-Grampion Expositions Group, 1983.

Conference on CAD/CAM Technology in Mechanical Engineering, 1982, Massachusetts Institute of Technology. *Proceedings*. Cambridge, MA: Massachusetts Institute of Technology, 1982.

Conference on Computer-Aided Manufacture, 1978, National Engineering Laboratory. *Proceedings*. Glasgow: National Engineering Laboratory, 1978.

Conference on Computer-Aided Manufacturing and Productivity, 1981, London. *CAMPRO '81.* London: Institution of Production Engineers, 1981.

Conference on Production Research and Technology. *Proceedings.* Washington, DC: National Science Foundation, 9th, 1981-   . Irregular.

European Conference on Automated Manufacturing, 3rd, 1985, Birmingham, UK. *Proceedings.* Kempston, Bedford, UK: IFS (Publications), Ltd., 1985.

EUROGRAPHICS International Conference and Exposition. *Proceedings.* New York: Elsevier North Holland, 1980-   . Annual.

Sponsored by the European Association for Computer Graphics; European counterpart to ACM's SIGGRAPH Conference.

European Conference on Computer-Aided Design in Medium Sized and Small Industries (MICAD), 2nd, 1982, Paris. *CAD in Medium Sized and Small Industries.* New York: North-Holland Pub. Co., 1982.

European Conference on Integrated Interactive Computing Systems, 1982, Stresa, Italy. *Proceedings.* New York: North-Holland Pub. Co., 1983.

Graphics Interface '85., 1985, Montreal. *Proceedings.* New York: Springer Verlag, 1985.

IFAC Workshop on Design of Work in Automated Manufacturing Systems, Karlsrubes, West Germany, 1983. *Proceedings.* New York: Pergamon Press, 1984.

Intergraphics '83, 1983, Tokyo. *Computer Graphics.* New York: Springer-Verlag, 1983.

International Computer Graphics Symposium, 1968, Brunel University. *Computer Graphics.* New York: Plenum, 1975, c1969.

International Conference Exhibition on the Use of Computers in Design Engineering, 4th, 1980, Brighton, UK. *Proceedings.* Guilford, UK: IPC Science and Technology, 1980.

International Conference on Assembly Automation, 5th, 1984, Kempston, UK. *Proceedings*. Bedford, UK: IFS (Publications), 1984.

International Conference on Automatic Assembly. *Proceedings*. Bedford, UK: IFS (Publications), 1980-   . Annual.

International Conference of Computer-Aided Design Education, 1977, Teeside Polytechnic. *CAD ED: Proceedings*. Guilford, England: IPC Science and Technology Press, 1977.

International Conference on Computer-Aided Design of Concrete Structures, 1984, Split Yugoslavia. *Proceedings*. Swansea, UK: Pineridge Press, 1984.

International Conference on Flexible Manufacturing Systems. *Proceedings*. Bedford, UK: IFS (Publications), 1982-   . Annual.

International Machine Tool Design Research Conference. *Proceedings*. (Formerly: *Advances in Machine Tool Design and Research*). New York: Macmillan Press, Ltd., 1960-   . Annual.

Joint Polytechnic Symposium on Manufacturing Engineering, 2nd, 1979, Lanchester Polytechnic. *Proceedings*. Guilford, England: IPC Science and Technology, 1977-   . Irregular.

Man-Computer Communications Seminar, 4th, 1975, Ottawa. *Proceedings*. Ottawa: National Research Council, 1975.

NASTRAN Users' Colloquium. *Proceedings*. Washington, DC: National Aeronautics and Space Administration, 1972-   . Annual.

National Computer Graphics Association. *Proceedings*. Fairfax, VA: National Computer Graphics Association, 1980-   . Annual.

Numerical Control Society. *Meeting and Technical Conference*. Glenview, IL: Numerical Control Society, 1963-   . Annual.

Worldwide Manufacturing Productivity Conference, 1980, Warren, MI. *Conference Proceedings and Papers*. Warren, MI: Manufacturing Staff, General Motors Technical Center, 1980.

Research and Trade Journals and Newsletters

Some of the periodicals listed include special issues, reports, or columns on CAD/CAM or compute graphics. This information is included for these periodicals.

ACM Transactions on Graphics. New York: Association for Computing Machinery, 1982-   . Quarterly.

Some issues include parts of the SIGGRAPH Annual Conference on Computer Graphics and Interactive Techniques Proceedings.

American Machinist & Automated Manufacturing. (Formerly: *American Machinist*.) New York: McGraw Hill, 1877-   . Monthly.

Special Report 770: Manufacturing Control Software. 129(10):113-132; 1985 October.

Special Report 772: The Interface Challenge: Report from the Committee on the CAD/CAM Interface. 129(1):95-116; 1985 January.

Special Report 775: Integrated QA: Closing on the CIM Loop. 129(4):137-160; 1985 April.

Special Report 777: America's Commitment to Manufacturing Education. 129(6):105-120; 1985 June.

The Anderson Report on Computer Graphics. Simi Valley, CA: Anderson Publishing, 1978-   . Monthly.

Automation and Remote Control. (Translation of *Avtomatikai Telemekhanika*). New York: Consultants Bureau, 1956-   . Semimonthly.

Byte: The Small Systems Journal. Peterborough, NH: McGraw-Hill, 1975-   . Monthly.

Special issue: Computer Graphics. 10(9); 1984 September.

CAD/CAM Alert. Chestnut Hill, MA: Management Roundtable, 1985-   . Monthly.

C.I.R.P. Annals. Berne, Switzerland: International Institution for Production Engineering Research, 1951-   . Annual.

CIM Review: The Journal of Computer-Integrated Manufacturing Management. Pennsauken, NJ: Auerbach Pub. Co., 1984-   . Quarterly.

CIM Strategies: *Computer-Integrated manufacturing*. Newton, MA: Cahners, 1984-   . Semimonthly.

CIM Technology. (Formerly: *CAD/CAM Technology*). Dearborn, MI: Society of Manufacturing Engineers, 1982-   . Quarterly.

Computer. New York: IEEE Computer Society, 1966-   . Monthly.
   Special issue: Practice and Progress in CAD/CAM. 17(12); 1984 December.

Computer-Aided Design. London: Butterworths, 1968-   . Bimonthly.
   Special issue: International yearbook 1985: A CAD Special Issue. 16(7); 1985 December.

Computer-Aided Design Report. San Diego, CA: CAD/CAM Publishing, Inc., 1981-   . Monthly.

Computer-Aided Engineering: Database Application Design and Manufacturing. Cleveland, OH: Penton/IPC Pub., 1982-   . Monthly.
   Special issue: Reference Manual. 4(11/12); 1985/1986 December/January.

Computer Design. Tulsa, OK. Advanced Technology Group of Pennwell Publication, 1962-   . Monthly.
   Special issue: Automation and Control. 22(4); 1983 April.
   Special Report on Graphics Systems Design Technology. 21(7):107-182; 1982 July.
   Special Report on Designing for Automation and Control. 21(11):161-220; 1982 November.
   Special report on Control and Automation. 20(11):109-194; 1981 November.

Computer Graphics: A Quarterly Report of ACM SIGGRAPH. New York: Association for Computing Machinery, vol. 6, 1972-   . Quarterly.

Computer Graphics News. New York: Scherago Associates Pub., Inc., 1981-   . Monthly.

Computer Graphics Forum. Amsterdam, The Netherlands: Elsevier Science Publishers, 1982-   . Quarterly.

Computer Graphics Technology Newsletter. Irvine, CA: Computer Graphics Technology, 1980-   . Monthly.

Computer Graphics Today. New York: Media Horizons, Inc., 1984-   . Monthly.

Computer Graphics World. San Francisco, CA: A PennWell Publication, 1978-   . Monthly.
   Special article: The Road to CIM. 8(11):21-28; 1985 November.

Computer Technology Review: *The Systems Integration Sourcebook.* Los Angeles: West World Publications, 1981-   . Quarterly.
   Special section: Computer Graphics, CAD/CAM and Image Processing.

Computer Vision, Graphics and Image processing. (Formerly: *Computer Graphics and Image Processing*). New York: Academic Press, 1972-   . Monthly.

Computerized Manufacturing. Conroe, TX: Technical Database Corp., 1983-   . Monthly.

Computers & Graphics: *An International Journal of Applications in Computer Graphics.* Elmsford, NY: Pergamon Press, 1975-   . Quarterly.

Computers and Industrial Engineering. Elmsford, NY: Pergamon Press, 1976-   . Quarterly.
   Includes software survey.
   Special issue: Computer Graphics. 9(1); 1985.

Computers in Industry: *An International Journal.* New York: Elsevier Science Publishers, 1979-   . Bimonthly.
   Special issue: International Aspects in CAD and CAM. 5(4): 1984/95 December/January.

Computers in Mechanical Engineering (CIME). New York: American Society of Mechanical Engineers, 1982-   . Bimonthly.
   Special issue: The Automation of Manufacturing. 2(4); 1984 January.
   Special issue: New Views in Color Graphics. 3(1); 1985 July.
   Special issue: Optimization in Manufacturing. 4(2); 1985 September.

Special issue: Computer-Integrated Manufacturing. 4(3); 1985 November.

Special issue: Integrated Software for CAE. 4(4); 1986 January.

Control Engineering. Barrington, IL: Technical Publishing Co., 1954-   . Monthly.

Design News. Newton, MA: Cahners Pub. Co., 1946-   . Semimonthly.

Special issue: Fluid Power: CAD/CAM. 40(4); 1984 February 20.

Special issue: Aerospace: CAD/CAM. 39(21); 1985 April 8.

Special issue: Design Awards: Computer & CAD/CAM. 39(21); 1985 November 7.

Displays: Technology and Applications. Surrey, UK: IPC Science and Technology Press, 1979-   . Quarterly.

Electronic Design. Hasbrouck Heights, NJ: Hayden Publishing Co., 1953-   . Biweekly.

Special issue: CAE/CAM. 31(33). 1983 November 10.

Special issue: CAE Software Modems. 32(25); 1984 December 13.

Special issue: Computer Graphics. 32(14); 1984 July 12.

High Technology. Boston: High Technology Publishing Corp., 1981-   . Monthly.

IBM Journal of Research and Development. Armonk, NY: IBM, 1957-   . Bimonthly.

Special issue: Computers in Manufacturing. 29(4); 1985 July.

IBM Technical Disclosure Bulletin. Armonk, NY: IBM, 1958-   . Monthly.

IEEE Computer Graphics and Applications. Los Alamitos, CA: IEEE Computer Society and National Computer Graphics Association. 1981-   . Monthly.

Special issue: *Integrating the Islands of Automation*. 5(2); 1985 February.

IEEE Expert Systems and Their Applications. Los Alamitos, CA: IEEE Computer Society, 1986-   . Quarterly.

IEEE Journal of Robotics and Automation. New York: Institute of Electrical and Electronics Engineers, Robotics and Automation Council 1985-   . Quarterly.

IEEE Transactions on Computer-Aided Design of Integrated Circuits and Systems. New York: Institute of Electrical and Electronics Engineers, 1982-   . Quarterly.
   Special issue: CAD Tools for Custom IC's. CAD-3(1); 1984 January.
   Special issue: Design Aids and Design Automation. CAD-4(4); 1985 July.

IEEE Transactions on Industry Applications. New York: Institute of Electrical and Electronics Engineers, 1965-   . Bimonthly.

IEEE Transactions on Microwave Theory and Techniques. New York: Institute of Electrical and Electronics Engineers, 1953-   . Monthly.

IEEE Transactions on Pattern Analysis and Machine Intelligence. New York: IEEE Computer Society, 1979-   . Bimonthly.

IEEE Transactions on Software Engineering. Los Alamitos, CA: IEEE Computer Society, 1982-   . Monthly.

Industrial Engineering. Norcross, GA: American Institute of Industrial Engineers, 1969-   . Monthly.

Industrial Robot. Kempston, Bedford, England: IFS (Publication), 1973-   . Monthly.

The International Journal of Advanced Manufacturing Technology. Kempston, Bedford, England: IFS (Publications), 1985-   . Quarterly.

International Journal of Machine Tool Design and Research. New York: Pergamon Press, 1961-   . Quarterly.

International Journal of Production. London: Taylor & Francis, 1961-   . Bimonthly.

International Journal of Robotics Research. Cambridge, MA: Massachusetts Institute of Technology, 1982-   . Quarterly.

Journal of Engineering for Industry: Transactions B of the American Society of Mechanical Engineers. New York: American Society of Mechanical Engineers, 1959-   . Quarterly.

Journal of Manufacturing systems. Dearborn, MI: Society of Manufacturing Engineers, 1982-   . Semiannual.

Journal of Robotic Systems. New York: John Wiley & Sons, 1984-   . Quarterly.

Machine Design. Cleveland, OH: Penton/IPC, 1929-   . Bimonthly.
    Special issue: CAD/CAM Reference Issue. 57(24); 1985 October 17.

Machinery and Production Engineering. Brighton, England: Machinery Publications, Co. 1965-   . Weekly.

Manufacturing Engineering. Dearborn, MI: Society of Manufacturing Engineering, 1975-   . Monthly.
    Series of articles: CAD/CAM Overview. 95(4):61-77; 1985 October.
    Series of articles: CAD/CAM. 95(3):67-82; 1985 September.

Manufacturing Technology Horizons. Lake Geneva, WI: Manufacturing Technology Press, 1982-   . Bimonthly.

Mechanism and Machine Theory. Elmsford, NY: Pergamon Press, 1972-   . Bimonthly.
    Special issue: Computer-Aided Mechanism Design. 20(4); 1984.

Microprocessors at Work: A Manager's Guide to CAD/CAM Robotics, FMS and Automated Control Systems. Oxford, England: Elsevier International Bulletins, 1979-   . Monthly.

Modern Machine Shop. Cincinnati, OH: Gardiner Publications. Inc., 1928-   . Monthly.
    Special issue: A CAD/CAM Checklist. 58(4); 1985 September.
    Special issue: FMS and CAM. 58(9); 1986 February.

Production Engineering. Cleveland, OH: Penton/IPC, 1954-   . Monthly.
    Special issue: Automation Reference Issue and Buyer's Guide. 33(1); 1986 January.

Special issue: Integrated Manufacturing Staff Report. 33(2):IM1-IM32; 1986 February.

Robotica: International Journal of Information, Education and Research in Robotics and Artificial Intelligence. Cambridge, England: Cambridge University Press, 1983-   . Quarterly.

Robotics Age. Peterborough, NH: Robotics Age, Inc., 1983- Monthly.

Robotics and Computer-Integrated Manufacturing. Elmsford, NY: Pergamon Press, 1984-   . Quarterly.

Robotics Today. Dearborn, MI: Society of Manufacturing Engineers, 1979-   . Bimonthly.

Robotics World. Atlanta, GA, Communications Channels, 1983-   . Monthly.

The S. Klein Newsletter on Computer Graphics. Sudbury, MA: Technology & Business Communications, Inc., 1979-   . Semimonthly.

Tooling and Production. Solon, OH: Huebner Publications, 1960-   . Monthly.

Monographs

Barr, Paul C. *CAD: Principles and Applications*. Englewood Cliffs, NJ: Prentice-Hall, 1985.

Bertoline, Gary R. *Fundamentals of CAD*. Albany, NY: Delmar Publishers, Inc., 1985.

Besant, Colin B. *Computer-Aided Design and Manufacture*. 2nd ed. New York: Halstead Press, 1983.

Canada, John R. and Edwards, Robert L. *Should We Automate Now, or, Evaluation of Computer Integrated Manufacturing Systems*. Raleigh, NC: Industrial Extension Service, School of Engineering, North Carolina State University, 1985.

Encarnacao, Jose and Schlechtendahl, Ernst G. *Computer-Aided Design Fundamentals and Systems Architecture*. New York: Springer-Verlag, 1983.

Garden, Yvon and Lucas, Michel. *Interactive Graphics in CAD*. New York: UNIPUB, 1984.

Gardiner, Keith M. *Systems and Technology for Advanced Manufacturing*. 1st ed. Dearborn, MI: Society of Manufacturing Engineers, 1983.

Gardner, Leonard B. *Automated Manufacturing*. Philadelphia, PA: American Society for Testing and Materials, 1985.

Goetsch, David L. *Introduction to Computer-Aided Drafting*. Englewood Cliffs, NJ: Prentice-Hall, 1983.

Groover, McKell P. *CAD/CAM: Computer-Aided Design and Manufacturing*. Englewood Cliffs, NJ: Prentice-Hall, 1984.

Harrington, Joseph, Jr. *Computer-Integrated Manufacturing*. Huntington, NY: Krieger Pub. Co., 1979.

Harrington, Joseph, Jr. *Understanding the Manufacturing Process*. New York: Marcel Dekker. 1984.

Hatvany, Jozsef. *Word Survey of CAM*. Stoneham, MA: Butterworth, 1983.

Kochan, Detlef, *CAM: Developments in Computer-Integrated Manufacturing*. 1985.

Krouse, John K. *What Every Engineer Should Know about Computer-Aided Design and Computer-Aided Manufacturing: The CAD/CAM Revolution*. New York: Marcel Dekker, 1982.

Newman, William M. and Sproull, Robert F. *Principles of Interactive Computer Graphics*. 2nd ed. New York: McGraw-Hill, 1979.

Pao, Y.C. *Elements of Computer-Aided Design and Manufacturing*. New York: Wiley, 1984.

Ray, Martin S. *Elements of Engineering Design: An Integrated Approach*. Englewood Cliffs, NJ: Prentice-Hall, 1985.

Smith, Donald, Lester Colwell, and Richard Wilson. *CAD/CAM International Delphi Forecast Conducted in the United States*. 1st ed. Dearborn, MI: Society of Manufacturing Engineers, 1980.

Taraman, Khalil. *CAD/CAM Integration and Innovations*. Dearborn, MI: Computer and Automated Systems Association of the SME, 1985.

Taraman, Khalil. *CAD/CAM Meeting Today's Productivity, Challenge*. 1st ed. Dearborn, MI: Computer and Automated Systems Association of the SME, 1985.

Yoskiowa, Hiroyuki, Keith Rathmill, and Jozsef Hatvany. *Computer-Aided Manufacturing: An International Comparison*. Washington, DC: National Academy Press, 1981.

Monographic Series

Entries are arranged alphabetically by series title. Individual volumes are listed alphabetically by title with publication date under the appropriate series title.

Society of Manufacturing Engineers. Technical Papers. Dearborn, MI: Society of Manufacturing Engineers.
Approximately 700 papers published each year from key presentations at SME conferences.

IDC's Computer Integrated Manufacturing Series. Framingham, MA: International Data Corp.
  The Automated Material Handling Systems. 1985.
  Industrial Control Systems Market Overview. 1984.
  Manufacturing Information Systems Overview. 1984.
  Use of CAD in the AEC Market. 1983.
  Use of CAD/CAM in the Mechanical Design Department. 1983.
  Use of CAD/CAM/CAE in the Electrical/Electronic Design Market. 1984.
  Use of CAE in Mechanical Design. 1984.
  Use of PLC's in Discrete and Batch Industries. 1985.

Computer Systems Engineering Series. New York: Crane, Russak & Co.
  Automata Theory: Fundamentals and Applications. 1975.
  Computer-Aided Design of Digital Systems. 1977.
  Computer-Interfacing and On-Line Operations. 1975.
  Interactive Computer Graphics. 1976.

Institution of Electrical Engineers. Conference Proceedings. Piscataway, NJ: Institution of Electrical Engineers.
   European Conference on Electronic Design Automation. 1984.
   International Conference on Computer-Aided Design. 1972.
   International Conference on the Development of Flexible Automation Systems. 1984.

International Trends in Technology Manufacturing Series. Kempston, Bedford, England: IFS (Publications).
   Flexible Manufacturing Systems. 1985.
   Programmable Assembly. 1984.
   Robot Sensors. 1986.
   Robot Vision. 1983.

The Kluwer International Series in Engineering. Boston: Kluwer Academic Publishing.
   Computer-Aided Design and VLSI Device Development. 1986.
   Machine Learning: A Guide to Current Research. 1986.
   Perceptual Organization and Visual Recognition. 1985.
   Shadows and Silhouettes in Computer Vision. 1985.

Manufacturing Engineering and Material Processing. New York: Marcel Dekker, 1977-   .
   Automatic Assembly. 1982.
   Computers in Manufacturing. 1977.
   Computer-Integrated Manufacturing. 1985.
   Improved Productivity Classification, Coding and Data Base Standardization: The Key to Minimizing CAD/CAM and Group Technology. 1981.
   Interface Technology for Computer-Controlled Manufacturing Processes. 1983.
   Manufacturing Engineering. 1985.
   Manufacturing Engineering Processes. 1982.
   Understanding Manufacturing. 1977.
   Understanding the Manufacturing Process. 1984.

Manufacturing Update Series. Dearborn, MI: Society of Manufacturing Engineers.
   Achieving Success in Manufacturing Management. 1980.
   CAD/CAM Integration and Innovations. 1985.

CAPP, Computer-Aided Processing Planning. 1985.
Flexible Manufacturing Systems. 1984.
Group Technology at Work. 1984.
Maintenance Management for Quality Production. 1984.
Manufacturing Cost Estimating. 1980.
Modern Trends in Cutting Tools. 1982.
Production Design Engineering for Quality Improvement. 1983.
Systems and Technology for Advanced Manufacturing. 1983.

Mechanical Engineering. New York: Marcel Dekker.
CAD/CAM Dictionary. 1985.
CAD/CAM Systems Planning and Implementation. 1983.
Computer-Aided Graphics and Design. 1979.
Computer-Aided Kinetics for Machine Design. 1981.
Design Dimensioning with Computer Graphics Applications. 1984.
Engineering Documentation for CAD/CAM Applications. 1984.
Optimal Engineering Design Principles and Applications. 1982.
Principles of Automated Drafting. 1984.

Productivity Equipment Series. Dearborn, MI: Society of Manufacturing Engineers.
CAD/CAM. 2nd ed. 1985.
CAD/CAM: Designing and Drafting CAD/CAM Systems. 1985.
Machine Vision. 1984.
Numerical Control. 1983.

Standards

Industrial and International Standards. Englewood, CO: Information Handling Services (IHS), 1920- . Bimonthly.
  Online vendor: BRS.

Military & Federal Specifications & Standards. Englewood, CO: Information Handling Services (IHS), 1983- . Bimonthly.
  Online vendor: BRS.

Standards & Specifications. Bethesda, MD: National Standards Association, 1950- . Monthly.
  Online vendor: DIALOG.

Voluntary Standards Information Network. Englewood, CO: Information Handling Services (IHS), 1983- . Biweekly.
  Online vendor: BRS.

Van Deusen, Edmund. *Graphics Standards Handbook*. Laguna Beach, CA: CC Exchange, 1985.
  Explanation of six major computer graphics standards which are either adopted or proposed; includes information on how to obtain copies of these standards.

Patents

CAD/CAM Abstracts. New York: EIC/Intelligence Pub. Div., 1984- . Monthly.
  Includes references to patents.

Catalog of Government Patents. Springfield, VA: National Technical Information Service, 1981- . Monthly.
  Republished from *Government Reports Announcement and Index*; includes "Machinery & Tools" and "Manufacturing & Tools" and "Manufacturing Processes" sections.

CLAIMS/U.S. PATENTS. Alexandria, VA: IFI/Plenum Data Co., 1963- . Weekly.
  Online vendors: DIALOG and SDC; Online counterpart to *Official Gazette of the United States Patent and Trademark Office*.

Index of Patents Issued from the United States Patents and Trademark Office. Washington, DC: U.S. Government Printing Office, 1920- . Annual.

JAPIO (Japanese Patents in English). Tokyo: Japan Patent Information Organization, 1977- . Monthly.
  Online vendor: SDC; References for Japanese patents, utility models, designs, and trademarks.

NASA Patent Abstracts Bibliography. Washington, DC: U.S. National Aeronautics and Aerospace Abstracts, 1972- . Semiannual.
  Patents republished from *Scientific and Technical Aerospace Reports*.

"New Patents Section," in *Mechanism and Machine Theory* vol. 19, no. 1, 1984- . Bimonthly.

Abstracts from Pergamon PATSEARCH database; document delivery included.

Official Gazette of the United States Patent and Trademark Office. Washington, DC: U.S. Government Printing Office, 1872- Weekly.

Online formats (vendors): *CLAIMS/US PATENTS* (DIALOG, SDC), *PATSEARCH* (Pergamon), *PATDATA* (BRS).

PATDATA. Latham, NY: BRS, 1975- . Weekly.

Online vendor: BRS; Online counterpart to *Official Gazette of the U.S. Patent and Trademark Office.*

The Patent Newsletters. Boston, MA: Communications Publishing Group, Inc. Monthly.

Series of monthly newsletters which lists U.S. and foreign patents; although no one newsletter is devoted specifically to patents in manufacturing or design, special newsletters are published for robotics, packaging, textiles, and other manufacturing fields; entries include citations, diagrams, and abstracts; document delivery is also offered.

(WPI): World Patents Index. Place: Derwent Pubs, Inc., 1963- . Weekly.

Online vendors: DIALOG, SDC; patents for 24 major countries.

PATSEARCH. McLean, VA: Pergamon Infoline, Inc., 1970- .Weekly.

Online vendor: Pergamon; Online counterpart to *Official Gazette of the United States Patent and Trademark Office.*

Software

Computer-Aided Design, Engineering and Drafting. Pennsauken, NJ: Auerbach Publishers, Inc., 1984- . Quarterly.

Computer-Aided Design Systems Update. Yonkers, NY: Engineering Software, 1986- . Monthly.

DATAPRO Directory of Microcomputer Software. Delran, NJ: DATAPRO Research, 1980- . 2 base volumes with monthly updates.

Flora, Philip, ed. *International CAD/CAM Software Directory*. Blue Ridge Summit, PA: TAB Books, Inc., 1986.

Low Cost CAD/CAM Systems: Computer-Aided Design. Yonkers, NY: Engineering Software Exchange, 1986- . Annual.

MENU – The International Software Database. Fort Collins, CO: International Software Database Corp., 1973- . Monthly.
   Online vendor: DIALOG

Online Microcomputer Software Guide and Directory. Weston, CT: Online, Inc., 1973- . Monthly.
   Online vendor: BRS.

Software Catalog: Science and Engineering. New York: Elsevier Science Publishing Co., 1984.
   Software packages for all major micro and minicomputers

International CAD/CAM Software Directory. Conroe, TX: Technical Database, 1985- . Monthly.
   Online vendor: Technical Database.

APPENDIX 3

ASSOCIATIONS AND SOCIETIES

The *Encyclopedia of Associations* and *Directory of Engineering Societies and Related Organizations* list organizations with interests in the CAD/CAM field. Used in its online format, *Encyclopedia of Associations* is an excellent way to identify organizations. The *Robotics, CAD/DAM Market Place* also lists associations.

American Institute for Design
   and Drafting
966 Hungerford Drive
Suite 10-B
Rockville, MD 20854

Association for Integrated
   Manufacturing Technology
111 E Wacker Drive
Suite 600
Chicago, IL 60601
312/644-6610

Computer Aided
Manufacturing-International
611 Ryan Plaza Drive
Suite 1107
Arlington, TX 76011
817/860-1654

Computer and Automated
Systems Association of the
SME
Box 930
One SME Drive
Dearborn, MI 48121
313/271-1500

European Association for
Computer Graphics
PO Box 16
1288 Aire-le-Ville
Geneva, Switzerland

IEEE Computer Society
1109 Spring Street
Suite 300
Silver Spring, MD 20910
301/589-8142

Institute of Industrial
Engineers
25 Technology Park
Atlanta, GA 30092
404/449-0460

International Federation for
Information Processing
IFIP Secretariat
3 rue du Marche
CH-1204 Geneva,
Switzerland
e 22-282649

International Institute for
Production Engineering
Research
(College Internationale Pour
"Etude Scientifique des
Techniques de Production
Mecanique)
19 rue Blanche
F-75009 Paris, France

National Computer Graphics
Association
8401 Arlington Blvd.
Fairfax, VA 22031
703/698-9600

Society for Computer
Applications in Engineering
Planning and Architecture
358 Hungerford Drive
Rockville, MD 20850
301/762-6070

Society of Manufacturing
Engineers
PO Box 930
One SME Drive
Dearborn, MI 48121
313/271-1500

Special Interest Group on
Computer Graphics and
Interactive Techniques c/o
Association for Computing
Machinery
11 W. 42nd Street, 3rd
Floor
New York, NY 10030
212/869-7440

World Computer Graphics
Association
2033 M Street, Suite 399
Washington, DC 20036
202/775-9556

RESEARCH CENTERS

These centers were selected from *Research Centers Directory* and *Government Research Directory*. The *Robotics, CAD/CAM Market Place*; *Computer Graphics Marketplace*; and *Scientific and Technical Organizations and Agencies Directory* also list research centers.

Air Force ICAM Program
  Directorate of Research and Development Contracting
  Aeronautical Systems Divisions
  Air Force Systems Command
  Department of the Air Force
  Wright-Patterson Air Force Base, OH 45433
  513/378-3895

Brigham Young University
  Computer Aided Manufacturing Laboratory
  265 Technology Building
  Provo, UT 84602
  801/378-3895

Carnegie-Mellon University
  SRC-CMU Research Center for Computer-Aided Design
  Pittsburgh, PA 15213
  412/578-8889

Cornell University
  Cornell Manufacturing Engineering and Productivity Program
  319 Upson Hall
  Ithaca, NY 14853
  607/256-4856

Illinois Institute of Technology
  10 West 35th Street
  Chicago, IL 60616
  312/567-4800

McMaster University
  Centre for Flexible Manufacturing Research and Development
  1280 Main Street
  Hamilton, ON Canada
  416/525-9140

Massachusetts Institute of
  Technology
  Laboratory for
  Manufacturing and
  Productivity
  Room 35-238
  77 Massachusetts Avenue
  Cambridge, MA 02139
  617/253-2234

National Science Foundation
  Mechanical Engineering
  and Applied Mechanics
  Division
  Production Research
  Program
  1800 G Street NW
  Washington, DC 20550

Ohio State University
  Manufacturing Systems
  Laboratory Complex
  Department of Industrial
  and Systems Engineering
  1971 Neil Avenue
  Columbus, OH 43210
  614/422-6239

Purdue University
  Center for CAD/CAM
  Room 1107
  799 W. Michigan Street
  Indianapolis, IN 46202
  317/264-8627

Rensselaer Polytechnic
  Institute
  Center for Manufacturing
  Productivity and
  Technology Transfer
  110 Eight Street
  Troy, NY 12180
  518/266-6724

United States Department of
  Commerce
  National Engineering
  Laboratory
  Center for Manufacturing
  Engineering

–Automated Manufacturing
  Research Facility
  Gaithersburg, MD 20899
  301/921-3421

–Fabrication Technology
  Division
  Bldg 304 Rm 136
  Gaithersburg, MD 20899

–Automated Production
  Technology
  Gaithersburg, MD 20899
  301/921-2577

University of California,
  Berkeley
  Electronics Research
  Laboratory
  Cory Hall
  Berkeley, CA 94720
  415/642-2301

University of Iowa
 Center for Computer-Aided
 Design
 1409 Engineering Building
 Iowa City, IA 42242
 319/353-8988

University of Michigan
 Center for Research in
 Integrated Manufacturing
 251 Chrysler Center
 Ann Arbor, MI 48109
 313/763-2174

University of Virginia
 Center for Computer-Aided
 Engineering
 School of Engineering and
 Applied Science
 Charlottesville, VA 22901
 804/924-6217

ONLINE VENDORS

BRS
 BRS Information
 Technologies
 1200 Route 7
 Latham, NY 12110
 800/833-4707;
 800/553-5566 (NY)

DIALOG Information
 Services, Inc.
 3460 Hillview Avenue
 Palo Alto, CA
 800/334-3564

INTIME Manufacturing
 DataBank
 Society of Manufacturing
 Engineers
 One SME Drive
 Dearborn, MI
 313/271-1500

Japan Patent Information
 Organization
 Bensui Building 1-5-16
 Toranoman
 Minato-ku
 Tokyo 105 Japan
 81(3) 503-6181

Orbit Information
 Technologies
 800 Westpark Drive
 McLean, VA 22102
 800/421-7229

Technical Database Online
 PO Box 720
 Conroe, TX 77305
 409/539-9688

WILSONLINE
 H.W. Wilson Company
 950 University Avenue
 Bronx, NY 10452
 800/367-6770

FIGURE 1

SUBJECT SEARCH - TI,ID,DE

(1981-1985, inclusive)

(percentage)

CAD/TI,ID,DE or COMPUTER( )AIDED( )DESIGN/TI,ID,DE

COMPENDEX	Ei Meetings	INSPEC	NTIS	The Computer Database*
4.55	6.85	5.63	2.797	6.03

COMPUTER( )AIDED( )MANUFACTUR?/TI,ID,DE

COMPENDEX	Ei Meetings	INSPEC	NTIS	The Computer Database*
1.01	3.56	0.147	0.885	0.407

CAD( )CAM/TI,ID,DE

COMPENDEX	Ei Meetings	INSPEC	NTIS	The Computer Database*
0.170	0.830	0.814	0.080	1.97

COMPUTER( )INTEGRATED( )MANUFACTUR?/TI,ID,DE

COMPENDEX	Ei Meetings	INSPEC	NTIS	The Computer Database*
0.062	0.58	0.174	0.011	0.030

*limited to 1982-1985 and TI,DE

FIGURE 2
SCISEARCH SUBJECT SEARCH RESULTS

Publication Papers	Number of Papers	Number of Cited Papers	Number of Citing Papers*
1977	5	5	1
1978	29	15	7
1979	41	74	18
1980	44	44	11
Total	119	138	37

*for a five year period subsequent to the publication date of the cited paper's publication date

FIGURE 3
Journal Titles from Original Subject Search

Occurance	Impact Factor	Journal Title
12	0.349	Computer-Aid Design
7	1.284	Computer and Graphics
5	0.000	Manufacturing Engineering
4	-	Design News
4	-	Engineering
4	0.174	Journal of Mechanical Design: Transactions B
4	0.042	Telecommunications and Radio Engineering
4	-	Astronautics and Aeronautics
3	0.132	Electronics
3	-	Engineering Materials and Design
3	1.211	IEEE Transactions on Microwave Theory and Techniques
3	0.016	Toshiba Review

FIGURE 4

Citing Journal Titles

Frequency of Citing	Impact Factor	Journal Title
24	1.211	IEEE Transactions on Microwave Theory and Techniques
19	2.342	IEEE Transactions of Electron Devices
15	0.342	Computer-Aided Design
12	1.004	IEEE Journal of Solid State Physics
12	0.355	Journal of Optimization Theory and Applications
7	1.132	Electronics
6	1.033	IEEE Transactions on Circuits and Systems
5	1.434	Applied Optics
5	0.950	British Journal of Opthalmology
5	0.422	International Journal of Circuit Theory and Applications
5	-	Philips Technical Review
4	-	Nachrichlentechnische Zeitschrift
3	0.821	Automatica
3	0.766	IEEE Transactions on Systems, Man and Cybernetics

FIGURE 5

Citing Journal Titles

Frequency of Citing	Impact Factor	Journal Title
15	1.211	IEEE Transactions on Microwave Theory and Techniques
10	2.342	IEEE Transactions on Electron Devices
9	1.033	IEEE Transactions on Circuits and Systems
8	-	IEEE Proceedings
5	1.327	Electronics Letters
5	0.882	IEE Proceedings D
5	0.462	IEE Proceedings G
4	1.668	IEEE Transactions on Computer-Aided Design of Integrated Circuits and Systems
4	0.847	IEEE Transactions on Sonics and Ultrasonics
3	1.004	IEEE Journal of Solid State Circuits
3	0.717	International Journal of Control
3	-	Philips Technical Review

NEW REFERENCE WORKS IN SCIENCE AND TECHNOLOGY

Robert G. Krupp, Editor

Reviewers for this column are: Amy D. Cooper (ADC), University of Vermont, Burlington, VT: Kerry L. Kresse (KLK), University of Kentucky, Lexington, KY; Robert G. Krupp (RGK), Maplewood, NJ; Barbara A. List (BL), University of Michigan, Ann Arbor, MI; and Ellis Mount (EM), Columbia University, New York, NY.

ENGINEERING AND TECHNOLOGY

(The) chemical engineering guide to heat transfer. Vol. 1. *Plant Principles.* Edited by Kenneth J. McNaughton and staff of *Chemical Engineering.* New York: Hemisphere; New York: McGraw-Hill; 1986. 362 p. $49.95. ISBN 0-89116-465-0 (Hemisphere); 0-07-606939-7 (McGraw Hill).

> This collection of 48 reprints was taken from pages of *Chemical Engineering* over the period 1979-85 (but mostly 1981) and covers the basic plant principles of heat transfer. Involved are all the different types of heat exchangers and how to select the right one, shell-and-tube equipment and how it works, design (calculator programs and modeling), heat recovery, steam (as the conveyor of heat), and cost (the bottom line). For chemical engineers in industry and academe (even if the library has been subscribing to *Chemical Engineering*). (RGK)

(The) chemical engineering guide to heat transfer. Vol. 2. *Equipment.* Edited by Kenneth J. McNaughton and staff of *Chemical Engineering.* New York: Hemisphere;

New York: McGraw-Hill; 1986. 300p. $49.50. ISBN 0-89116-466-9 (Hemisphere); 0-07-606940-0 (McGraw Hill).

> This is a companion to Volume 1 and contains 45 reprints covering 1979-1985 (but mostly 1983) from *Chemical Engineering*. Here are reports on the equipment involved with heat transfer. Putting theory to the test, discussions include how boilers work, the cooling process, heating (insulation and winterizing), condensers (with a calculator program), and a pot pourri of other equipment (even including solar ponds). For all chemical engineering libraries (even those with subscriptions to *Chemical Engineering*). (RGK)

Complete handbook of electric motor controls. By John E. Traister. Englewood Cliffs, NJ: Prentice-Hall; 1986. 279 p. $24.95. ISBN 0-13-160938-6.

> Provides up-to-date information on therapy, design, and practical applications as an aid to all concerned with electric and electronic motor controls. Applications covered involve motors in residential, commercial, and industrial installations. Well-illustrated. There is also an excellent appendix of almost 500 classified trade sources. (RGK)

Construction hazard and safety handbook. By R. W. King and R. Hudson. Boston: Butterworths; 1985. 477p. $89.95. ISBN 0-408-01347-8.

> This work focuses on the hazards to safety and health of workers in a wide range of construction trades and occupations. Sound and timely advice is provided, with the authors encouraging the construction industry rather than government to look for real and lasting improvement. Though the overall tone of the book is based on British examples and experience, it is worth shelf space in all construction engineering collections. (RGK)

Dictionary of biotechnology. By J. Coombs. New York: Elsevier; 1986. 330p. $39.50. ISBN-0-444-01087-4 (pbk).

> Biotechnology is defined, in part, in this dictionary as "the application of organisms, biological systems or biological processes to manufacturing and service industries." The dictionary fills a void in this rapidly developing field. There are more than 3,000 definitions and numerous cross references. Terms not found elsewhere can be found here. Recommended for general academic and all kinds of science collections. (ADC)

Electrical engineering: the second century begins. Edited by Harlow Freitag. NY: IEEE Press; 1986. 180p. $27.50. ISBN 0-87942-208-4.

This book is an outgrowth of the 1984 centennial celebration of the Institute of Electrical and Electronics Engineers. To mark that date in a lasting fashion the editor has gathered together some material honoring past notables and other papers that present a picture of the future. The work of several dozen inventors and engineers is depicted in one section, followed by a review of Centennial activities, then come 21 papers on such topics as engineering education, computer evolution, future trends in components and future factories. It is an attractive, well-prepared book which should serve as a reliable reference work. (EM)

(The) electroplater's handbook. By C. W. Ammen. Blue Ridge Summit, PA: TAB; 1986. 213p. $18.95. ISBN 0-83-6-0410-3.

This is a hands-on, do-it-yourself book for the novice electroplater. It requires only a minimum of expenditure and no previous knowledge of the subject or of the chemistry involved. Well-illustrated. Best for personal purchase and public libraries. (RGK)

Evaporative air conditioning handbook. 2d ed. By John R. Watt. New York: Chapman and Hall; 1986. 455p. $54.50. ISBN 0-412-01151-4.

This new work reflects the growing interest in evaporative air conditioning since the 1963 edition. It shows how evaporative cooling will cost 50-75% less than electrical air cooling for installation, maintenance, and operation. Heavily illustrated. For a broad spectrum of contractors, manufacturing and design engineers, and government agencies concerned with energy or cooling. Also excellent for larger public libraries. (RKG)

Guidebook for electrical inspection. By John T. Earl. Englewood Cliffs, NJ: Prentice-Hall; 1986p. $27.95. ISBN 0-13-371360-1.

This is essentially an updated version of John E. Traister's *Electrical inspection guidebook* published in 1979 and covers regulations changed to reflect today's National Electrical Code. Included are descriptions of inspection duties, checklists, and correlation of construction inspection with successful management procedures. Provides appropriate illustrative matter. For personal purchase by anyone in the electrical construction industry, electrical engineering library collections, and larger public libraries. (RGK)

Handbook of modern electronics and electrical engineering. Edited by Charles Belove. New York: Wiley; 1986. 2401p. $85.00. ISBN 0-471-09754-3.

This reference work is designed to provide service to engineers in fields other than electronics, to practicing electrical and electronic engineers, and to management personnel. The 69 chapters provide an overview of each subject area plus basic theory and design information (as appropriate). Extensive bibliographies. There are three major parts involved: (1) mathematics, properties of materials and components; (2) electronic and electric circuits; and (3) systems. For most comprehensive science and technology collections. (RGK)

Handbook of pattern recognition and image processing. Edited by Tzay Y. Young and King-Sun Fu. New York: Academic; 1986. 705p. $89.00. ISBN 0-12-774560-2.

A reference work which provides a broad overview of the major elements of pattern recognition and image processing. Of the many applications discussed there are included character recognition, target detection, remote sensing, reliability analyses, speech recognition, and automatic inspection. These are primarily included in Part IV, whereas Parts I, II, and III are devoted to techniques, developments, and computer systems. Excellent documentation. For industrial engineers. (RGK)

Heat exchanger sourcebook. Edited by J. W. Palen. New York: Hemisphere; 1986. 805p. $59.95. ISBN 0-89116-451-0.

A collection of reprints from four very detailed works on heat exchangers in order to provide a single volume covering a less sweeping range of subjects. The editor selected articles which represented methods, data, or concepts directly useful without further development in the design or specification of process heat exchangers. Stress is placed on the practical use of available computational capabilities. For all serious engineering collections in industry and academe. (RGK)

(An) illustrated guide to modern trains. By Brian Hollingsworth. New York: Acro; 1985. 233p. $11.95. ISBN 0-668-06495-1.

Over the some 40 years since the end of World War II the cycle of steam locomotives to diesel, diesel-electric, and electric is moving once again (but a bit hesitatingly) back to steam. The guide traces this somewhat cyclic set of developments through text (minimal but not skimpy, and very factual) supplemented by glorious, magnificent illustrations, mostly in full color, by noting the world's most important and interesting locomotives built since 1945. Some aspects of trains themselves are included but they are not the prime concern. Eighty powerful locomotives form the base of this rare and yet timely compilation. Despite the fact that railroad technical jargon is heavily used throughout, thus making the work a joy for the true railway buff, the reference volume is very appropriate for public libraries and special collections on railroading. And for the price, it is a steal for personal purchase. (RGK)

Power plant evaluation and design reference guide. Edited by Tyler G. Hicks. New York: McGraw-Hill; 1986. Mixed pagination. $44.50. ISBN 0-07-028794-5.

In meeting the need for an up-to-date work covering the entire field of power plant design, this book draws heavily from quite recently published works and articles. Each of the reprints, carefully cited, is preceded by a brief introduction by the editor. For a broad spectrum of engineers who may require this design data for industrial or utility plants. Well-indexed. (RGK)

Shaft alignment handbook. By John Piotrowski. New York: Marcel Dekker; 1986. 278p. $59.50. ISBN 0-8247-7432-9.

This handbook is meant to consider shaft alignment questions for mechanics, foremen, technicians, and engineers. It shows how to properly align the shafts of two or more pieces of rotating equipment, thus minimizing vibration and reducing wear. Actually the work is a rather erudite training manual and handles all the problems in a careful, detailed manner. Patience and accuracy are watchwords. Heavily and appropriately illustrated. Bibliography quite current. Author with General Electric Co., Cincinnati. (RGK)

Timber construction manual. 3d ed., 1985. American Institute of Timber Construction. New York: Wiley; 1986. Mixed pagination. $39.95. ISBN 0-471-82758-4.

This new edition provides an update of the AITC Timber Construction Manual and reflects timber design methods. Part I contains general design data and construction information; Part II has information on loads and the design of structural elements and their fastenings; and Part III contains detailed reference information and recommended standards and specifications for engineered timber construction. For architects, engineers, and contractors interested in the laminating and fabricating industry. (RGK)

Trolley treasures. Vol. 1: The wartime years in New Jersey. By A. W. Mankoff and C. D. Wrege. Published by Railhead Publications, P.O. Box 526, Canton, Ohio 44701 and copyrighted by A. W. Mankoff in 1986. $14.95. 128p. ISBN 0-912113-26-X.

This work is indeed a true treasure of over 400 never-published black and white photographs of the last gasp of Public Service Coordinated Transport streetcars 2600-2699 (with Compromise Roof) during the wartime (WW II) years in New Jersey (exclusively the Essex and Hudson Divisions). Volumes 2 and 3 will have photos of the 2700s and the 3200s in Essex and Hudson counties and Camden, New Jersey. Except for some descriptive front matter, the "meat" of the work are photos sequentially arranged by car number (starting with 2600). Most of the tableaux show a car in actual service on lines in Newark (including its subway) and environs but there are some carbarn shots and a most unique

HEALTH SCIENCES

(The) best in medicine: where to get the finest health care for you and your family. By Herbert J. Dietrich and Virginia H. Biddle. New York: Harmony Books; 1986. 211p. $12.95. ISBN 0-517-55966-8.

The purpose of this book is to provide a guide to the "best" medical centers. (It does not claim to be exhaustive.) These "best" were determined by questionnaires sent to doctors, supplementary interviews, and statistics on postgraduate medical training programs. Thirteen chapters focus on specific areas of medicine such as cancer, geriatrics, psychiatry, etc. Each chapter begins with an overview of the specific medical field, followed by the recommended treatment centers. The overviews provide good, introductory information and, while the lists of recommended centers are open to differences of opinion, the patient seeking guidance will get it. It's fun to read. Recommended for medical, hospital, and public libraries. (ADC)

Catalog of teratogenic agents. 5th ed. By Thomas H. Shepard. Baltimore: Johns Hopkins University Press; 1986. 710p. $45.00. ISBN 0-8018-3350-7.

Of the more than 900 agents listed in this fifth edition, approximately 204 are new agents. Many nonteratogenic agents have been included because of the importance of negative published data. The main purpose of the catalog is to connect the information on experimental teratogenic agents with congenital defects in human beings. The catalog is arranged alphabetically by the name of the agent. The chemical name as it is listed in *The Merck Index* is used as the main entry. Trade names are listed as synonyms. Chemical Abstract numbers are included in the entry. There are extensive author and subject indexes. The subject index includes the synonyms used for an agent. This valuable reference tool is recommended for medical, pharmaceutical, chemical, and larger academic libraries. (ADC)

Dictionary of pharmacology. By W. C. Bowman et al. Boston: Blackwell Scientific Publications; 1986. 234p. $22.50. ISBN 0-632-01131-9.

This is a glossary of terms relevant to pharmacology. Names of drug classes are included, but individual drug names are not. Concepts which are not strictly pharmacological, but which are used by pharmacologists, have been included. The authors have tried to use the accepted meaning of a term and explain its origin. Reference to the original source is given in many of the entries. The value of this work is in the definitions themselves which provide a background in which the terms exist. Recommended for most health science collections. (ADC)

Drugs in pregnancy and lactation: a reference guide to fetal and neonatal risk. 2d ed. By Gerald G. Briggs and others. Baltimore: Williams & Wilkins; 1986. 537p. $47.95. ISBN 0-683-01058-1.

This reference guide lists more than 500 drugs in alphabetical order by the most commonly used generic name. Each drug monograph has six fields of information: U.S. generic name, pharmacologic class (e.g., antihistamines), risk factor during pregnancy (based on a Food and Drug Administration coding system), fetal risk summary (brief literature review), breast feeding summary (brief literature review), and references. An appendix lists the drugs in alphabetical order by pharmacologic class and an excellent index provides cross references from trade and foreign names. Recommended for biomedical, hospital, and pharmaceutical libraries. (ADC)

Encyclopedia of medical history. By Roderick E. McGrew. New York: McGraw-Hill; 1985. 400p. $34.95. ISBN 0-07-045087-0.

As a first step in information gathering, this encyclopedia will be a good source for general readers or students of the history of medicine. Each essay addresses an important medical topic, and varies in length from one to several pages. A list of sources for additional reading is appended to each discussion. Although there are no biographical entries as such, individuals' contributions are included as appropriate. Particular focus is placed on the history of diseases, treatment techniques, and instrumentation. The index is extensive and therefore helpful for locating material. This will be a good addition for both general and medical collections. (BL)

Guide to the literature of pharmacy and the pharmaceutical sciences. By Theodora Andrews. Littleton, CO: Libraries Unlimited; 1986. 383p. $37.50. ISBN 0-87287-420-6. (Reference sources in science and technology series)

The scope of this comprehensive, annotated bibliography by a Purdue University librarian is all of pharmacy. Part I covers reference books and they are well-represented (396 of 958 entries). The reference works are arranged by type of work, e.g., dictionaries. Part II covers textbooks and treatises arranged by broad subject areas, e.g., drug abuse. The third section covers databases and periodicals. Citations are complete and the annotations are informative. There are thorough author/title and subject indexes. Recommended for most health science collections. (ADC)

Medical abbreviations: 4200 conveniences at the expense of communications and safety. 3d ed. Compiled by Neil M. Davis. Huntington Valley, PA: Neil M. Davis Associates; 1987. 102p. $5.95. ISBN 0-931431-03-4.

> This handy, pocket-size listing of 4200 medical abbreviations, acronyms, and symbols has more than doubled the number of entries since it was first published in 1983 (with 1,700 abbreviations). It is an aid for those who read medical records and/or prescriptions. Recommended for medical and hospital libraries. (ADC)

(The) patient's guide to medical tests. 3d ed. By Cathey Pinckney and Edward R. Pinckney. New York: Facts On File; 1986. 385p. $21.95. ISBN 0-8160-1593-7 (pbk).

> The guide describes 1,063 medical tests of which 345 are new to this third edition. The tests are listed in alphabetical order under the most commonly used name and there are cross references from alternative names. For each test, the book includes a description of the procedure and the purpose; what the normal and abnormal values are; what an abnormal value might indicate; risk factors; pain or discomfort involved; cost range; and an accuracy and significance rating. Written for the lay reader. Highly recommended for medical, hospital, and public libraries. (ADC)

World guide to English speaking medical schools. By David M. Tarlow. St. Louis, MO: Datar Pub. Co.; 1986. 26p. $13.95. ISBN not available.

> This small paperback is a worldwide listing of medical schools in which English is the language of instruction. The listings are arranged alphabetically by country. The guide also includes a listing of Mexican medical schools because of the large number of Americans who attend them. Recommended for all medical libraries and larger academic collections. (ADC)

LIFE SCIENCES

(A) bibliography of termite literature 1966-1978. Compiled by E. Ernst and R. L. Araujo. New York: Wiley; 1986. 903p. $95.00. ISBN 0-471-90466X.

> This annotated bibliography is the link between two completely separate publications. The first is T. E. Snyder's *Annotated subject-heading bibliographies, 1350 BC to AD 1965*, published in various parts from 1956-1968 by the Smithsonian Institution. The second is *Termite Abstracts*, first published in 1980 by the Center for Overseas Pest Research/Tropical Development and Research Institute, and which is not published by Taylor & Francis Ltd. As such, it contains 3,165 items published in books, journals, and conferences proceedings between 1966-1978. The annotations, generally 100-200 words in length, are thoughtfully added for researchers in the tropics who do not always have access to strong research collections. Prices are even added in some instances,

though this feature will be of limited use. The entries are arranged by first author, and contain standard bibliographic data. An author index for additional authors is provided for cross-referencing. The extensive subject bibliography (349 pages in length) contains geographic entries, pesticides, insecticides, and scientific and common names in addition to regular subjects. However, cross-referencing in the subject index is limited, and scientific names tend to be the primary entries. Recommended for entomology collections in academic and special libraries. (KLK)

Birds: a guide to the literature. By Melanie Ann Miller. New York: Garland Publishing; 1986. 887p. $100.00. ISBN 0-8240-8710-0. (Garland Reference Library of the Humanities; 680.)

In compiling this annotated bibliography of bird literature, the author aimed to facilitate access to a vast body of material. The volume is impressive of the breadth of materials covered: general works such as dictionaries and catalogs; titles on behavior, ecology, photography, song, and many other subjects; species and group studies; area studies; field guides; children's literature; biographies; and fiction. A list of journals, periodicals, and organization publications is appended. Coverage of some titles is selective—those commonly found in bird bibliographies, for example, are not necessarily repeated. The annotations give scope, geographic coverage, a concise description, data on illustrations, and notes on special features. A name index aids in locating individuals as authors or subjects. (BL)

Collins guide to the insects of Britain and Western Europe. By Michael Chinery. London: Wm. Collins Sons & Co., Ltd.; 1986. 320p. $16.64. ISBN 0-00-219170-9.

Claiming to be the most extensive guide to insects of Britain and Western Europe, Chinery has compiled information regarding size, coloring, habitat, behavior, and food of many of them. There are nearly 100,000 known insect species in Europe, and no attempt was made here to include all of them. Rather, the intent of the book is to help the amateur identify members of the various families, choosing from the 100,000 species the ones most likely to be noticed because of size, color, habits, etc. More than 2,000 insects are illustrated, and the quality of these illustrations is excellent. The book is well organized, the key is easy to use, and the indexes are helpful. Recommended for academic and public libraries, and even though collections may not extend to European insects, the relatively low price makes it a good purchase. (KLK)

(The) complete guide to trees of Britain and northern Europe. By Alan F. Mitchell. Surrey, England: Dragon's World; 1985. 208p. ISBN 1850298-000-2. (price unknown)

The trees included in this volume are supposed to represent all the common and frequently seen trees of the region plus a wide selection of uncommon and rare species. Nearly 500 species and 250 varieties are covered. David More, the illustrator, has depicted them in typical landscapes, and has paid particular attention to identifying details such as bark, flowers, fruit, and shoots. He has also shown winter and summer appearance. The text covers the origin, history, distribution, and growth of the trees. A unique feature is the data on dimensions of giant and rare specimens. The last section gives advice on choice and cultivation of trees, including guidelines on planting, pruning, and measuring height. It also lists important tree collections. The index lists common name, followed by scientific name. (BL)

(The) concise birds of Britain and Europe: an illustrated checklist. By Hermann Heinzel. London: Hodder and Stoughton; 1985. 64p. $2.95. ISBN 0-340-37213-3.

This little volume was designed to provide a list of all the birds of Europe, yet be small enough for a birder to carry around comfortably. Organization is by family, within which birds are listed by common name. Henizel has drawn color pictures of all the birds, illustrating differences in females, winter plumage, and regional subspecies when significant. A distribution map is provided for all entries, along with a note on the status and frequency of occurrence in Britain and Ireland. Short descriptions cover any distinctive features and habits. At the back of the book, a list of "accidental and rare vagrants" is provided. Finally, there is an index of scientific names and an index of English common names. While meant to be a field guide, the book will be of value to any collection covering ornithology. (BL)

(The) encyclopedia of reptiles and amphibians. Edited by Tim R. Halliday and Kraig Adler. New York: Facts on File Publications; 1986. 159p. $24.95. ISBN 0-8160-1359-4.

This is another in a line of beautifully illustrated animal life encyclopedias issuing from the publisher recently. The initial color photograph of a White's tree frog making it closely resemble an extra from a Star Wars scene sets the pace for fantastic pictures. The following photographs, drawings, diagrams, and charts are of high quality and add immeasurably to the book's value. Introductory articles describe the two classes, followed by articles dealing with an order's physiological forms and niche diversity. Separate descriptions cover families, and emphasize different genera and species. The articles have been written by experts in the field of herpetology. More data are provided regarding numbers of genera and species in a family, general distribution, sizes, colors, and distinctive life stages. Symbols have been assigned to indicate the IUCN status in regard to species survival. A bibliography is provided, along with an index of scientific and common names. (BL)

(A) dictionary of genetic engineering. By Stephen G. Oliver and John M. Ward. New York: Cambridge University Press; 1985. 153p. $19.95. ISBN 0-521-26080-9.

Although a slim volume, this dictionary goes a long way toward providing a current list of terms utilized in a fast-moving field. The authors, both biochemists, have written clear and concise definitions for the specialized terms of genetic engineering. When appropriate, an example of usage is given. A smattering of useful illustrations is also included. One of the best features are its appendices: a list of restriction enzymes; restriction maps and DNA size markers; genetic nomenclature; genetics maps of *Escherichia coli* and *Saccharomyces ceravisiae*; the genetic code; and the one-and three-letter abbreviations for amino acids. (BL)

(The) encyclopedia of aquatic life. Edited by Keith Banister and Andrew Campbell. New York: Facts on File Publications; 1985. 372p. $35.00. ISBN 0-8160-1257-1.

The high standard set by the publisher's recent titles *The Encyclopedia of Mammals* and *The Encyclopedia of Birds* is met with this newest encyclopedia. Divided into three sections covering fishes, aquatic invertebrates, and sea mammals, its purpose is to provide information on groups that are totally aquatic. Each of the sections is preceded by a general essay that describes the group in broad terms. The articles that follow discuss phyla and classes in terms of natural history. Sidebars contain data on distribution, classification, and size. The illustrations are outstanding. Color photographs tend to depict interesting or typical behaviors, while the drawings, distribution maps, and anatomical diagrams offer much not covered in the articles. There is a glossary in addition to a bibliography, and the index lists common and scientific names. (BL)

Floristic regions of the world. By Armen Takhtajan. Translated by Theodore J. Crovello. Berkeley: University of California Press; 1986. 522p. $60.00. ISBN 0-520-04027-9.

This is a revised and expanded edition of *The Floristic Regions of the World* published in 1978 by Soviet Sciences Press. In particular, it contains a substantially expanded section on temperate North America. The purpose of this work is to provide a record of floristic geography on a worldwide basis. By establishing the geographic distribution of the planet's genetic resources, one has a database on which to base a global strategy for protecting those resources. Takhtajan has included a list of families of living vascular plants which indicates approximate number of genera and species of each family and its geographical distribution. This list is a revision of two previous versions. He has also revised a map of floristic regions and kingdoms. The list of references is arranged according to geographical divisions. (BL)

Sea mammals. Edited by David Macdonald. New York: Torstar Books; 1984. 158p. $35.00. ISBN 0-920269-75-3. (All the World's Animals.)

Dwellers of the world's oceans and seas are the subject of this encyclopedic work. It aims to give the reader the newest information about sea mammals in a manner both informative and entertaining. The work is directed to a wide audience that spans from professionals to high school students. The articles were prepared by experts in the field. A general essay introduces the text by discussing common features and variations in the biology, ecology, and behavior of sea mammals. This is followed by essays describing each order. Information covers distribution, a summary of species or species groupings, and a description of the skull, dentition, and other unusual skeletal features. The main body of the text proceeds to describe at the family level. Physical features, distribution, evolutionary history, diet and feeding behavior, social dynamics and spatial organization, classification, conservation, and relationships with man are all discussed. The text is enhanced by excellent photographs and drawings. In all, 113 species are described. A glossary is appended. The index lists animals by both common and scientific name. (BL)

PHYSICAL SCIENCES

Copper, silver, gold and zinc, cadmium, mercury oxides and hydroxides. Edited by T. P. Dirkse, New York: Pergamon; 1986. 360p. $100.00. ISBN 0-08-032497-5. (Solubility data series. Vol. 23.)

This reference work presents and evaluates data for the oxides and hydroxides of two groups of transition series metals from Groups I and II of the Periodic Table. Literature sources include *Chemical Abstracts* 1907-1984, Gmelin, *Handbuch der Anorganischen Chemie* prior to 1907, and the work of Mellor. However, with few exceptions, no works published before 1900 were used for preparing the 342 data sheets. Indexes include ones for the system, registry number, and authors. For all serious chemistry collections in industry and academe. (RGK)

Data for biochemical research. 3d ed. Edited by Rex M. C. Dawson and others. New York: Oxford University Press; 1986. 580p. $59.00. ISBN 0-19-855358-7.

A rather general collection of data on compounds required by the average biochemist. (Carefully complete so to avoid materials needed only by specialists in individual areas.) Thus the work is concise enough (over 4,000 compounds) for laboratory use. Arrangement is essentially by chemical categories (e.g., phosphate esters excluding nucleotides and coenzymes; steroids; pharmacologically active compounds). For collections on biological chemistry. (RGK)

Handbook of glass properties. By Narottam P. Bamsal and R. H. Doremus, New York: Academic; 1986. 680p. $135.00. ISBN 0-12-078140-9.

This is a collection of critically selected and correlated data on silicate glasses, but commercial glasses from European and Japanese manufacturers, nonsilicate glasses, for example, have been slighted. Scores of tables and figures of the most recent data are include: there is very strong bibliographic support. For reference collections in most science and technology libraries in industry and academe. (RGK)

Handbook of infrared standards with special maps and transition assignments between 3 and 2600 μm. By Guy Guelachvili and K. Narahari Rao. New York: Academic; 1986. 851p. $75.00. ISBN 0-12-305360-9.

This handbook provides lists of infrared standards based on spectra of easily available molecular species which should help investigators find wavenumber standards suitable for their particular research. The authors started at the upper end of the microwave region and stopped arbitrarily at 3000 cm^{-1}. The format used for the 425 main entries is not uncommon: the left-hand page contains a spectral map, with the wavenumber data on the right-hand page. A collection of 25 miscellaneous information tables precedes the handbook proper. For currently operating laboratories conducting studies in molecular spectroscopy. (RGK)

Handbook of magnetic phenomena. By Harry E. Burke. New York: Van Nostrand; 1986. 423p. $49.50. ISBN 0-442-21184-8.

Provides coverage of a startling number of different magnetic phenomena in order to help answer for technically oriented individuals the question: what are the electronic consequences when material and energy interact in the presence of magnetic fields? Thus, when contemplating a particular device, one can know what to expect from its use, both in performance and in limitations. The work, though indeed a handbook, is not constructed in that manner. It is very heavily illustrated but strangely without documentation. For physics collections, especially as concerning magnetism. Author's affiliation not provided. (RGK)

(The) laser guidebook. By Jeff Hecht. New York: McGraw-Hill; 1986. 381p. $49.50. ISBN 0-07-027733-8.

This is a work devoted to the functional characteristics of commercial lasers. It is neither a physics text nor a tabulation of laser lines. However, it is both tutorial and reference in content. There are a few overview chapters but the bulk of the chapters concern 18 kinds of lasers, and each of these chapters has a common structure to make reference use easier. There is also a table of commercial lasers organized by wavelength. Some of these data originally appeared in *Lasers and Applications* magazine. For all comprehensive physical science collections. (RGK)

Mathematical formulae for engineering and science students. By S. Barnett and T. M. Cromin. 4th ed. New York: Longman Scientific and Technical, co-published in the U.S., by Wiley; 1986. 77p. $9.95. ISBN 0-582-44758-5 (pbk.)

A new edition which continues to provide most of the commonly used mathematical formulas at university and college level in a compact and easy to use form. However, there are new sections on z-transforms, matrix algebra, and orthogonal polynomials and Walsh functions. Tables of logarithms and other functions are omitted and replaced with some frequently used statistical tables. Best for personal purchase. Both authors with University of Bradford (U.K.). (RGK)

N.B.: Given below are citations for a set of 10 Chapman and Hall Chemistry Sourcebooks. The review following the tenth book's citation is a general one covering the entire set.

Organometallic compounds of cobalt, rhodium and iridium. Edited by C. White. New York: Chapman and Hall; 1985. 291p. $40.00. ISBN 0-412-26800-0 (Pbk). (Chapman and Hall Chemistry Sourcebooks).

Organometallic compounds of zinc, cadmium and mercury. Edited by J. L. Wardell. New York: Chapman and Hall; 1985. 207p. $33.00. ISBN 0-412-26870-1 (pbk). (Chapman and Hall Chemistry Sourcebooks)

Organometallic compounds of nickel, palladium, platinum, copper, silver, and gold. Edited by R. J. Cross and D. M. Mingos. New York: Chapman and Hall; 1985. 333p. $40.00. ISBN 0-412-26840-X (pbk). (Chapman and Hall Chemistry Sourcebooks)

Organometallic compounds of boron. Edited by K. Smith. New York: Chapman and Hall; 1985. 304p. $40.00. ISBN 0-412-26790-X (pbk). (Chapman and Hall Chemistry Sourcebooks)

Organometallic compounds of alumimum, gallium, indium and thallium. Edited by A. McKillop and others. New York: Chapman and Hall; 1985. 309p. $40.00. ISBN 0-412-26780-2 (pbk). (Chapman and Hall Chemistry Sourcebooks)

Organometallic compounds of ruthenium and osmium. Edited by G. R. Knox. New York. Chapman and Hall; 1985. 283p. $40.00. ISBN 0-412-26850-7 (pbk). (Chapman and Hall Chemistry Sourcebooks)

Organometallic compounds of iron. Edited by G. R. Knox. New York: Chapman and Hall; 1985. 477p. $49.95. ISBN 0-412-26820-5 (pbk). (Chapman and Hall Chemistry Sourcebooks)

Organometallic compounds of the lanthanides, actimides and early transition metals. Edited by D. J. Cardin and others. New York: Chapman and Hall; 1985. 400p. $49.95. ISBN 0-412-26830-2 (pbk). (Chapman and Hall Chemistry Sourcebooks)

Organometallic compounds of silicon. Edited by D. R. M. Walton. New York: Chapman and Hall; 1985. 318p. $40.00. ISBN 0-412-26860-4 (pbk). (Chapman and Hall Chemistry Sourcebooks)

Organometallic compounds of germanium, tin, and lead. Edited by P. G. Harrison. New York: Chapman and Hall; 1985. 180p. $33.00. ISBN 0-412-26810-8 (pbk). (Chapman and Hall Chemistry Sourcebooks)

These ten volumes comprise a set, each one of which provides carefully tailored information for those concerned with specialized areas of chemistry, particularly organometallic compounds, Data have been taken from the primary literature up to mid-1983, but it should be noted that these sourcebooks have been reproduced for the most part from the *Dictionary of organometallic compounds* (its 1984 edition in three volumes). Each sourcebook volume has three indexes: a name index, a molecular formula index, and a CAS registry number index listing all CAS numbers included in that particular sourcebook in serial order. Eventually supplements to these sourcebooks will also be published. Purchase for laboratory or office use is best though the full *Dictionary* may be in the library. (RGK)

Table of radioactive isotopes. By Edgardo Browne and Richard B. Firestone. New York: Wiley; 1986. Mixed pagination. $59.95. ISBN 0-471-84909-X.

This massive and highly detailed work should satisfy the demand for *adopted* properties of *all* radiations emitted by nuclei. Some of the properties were derived from experimental data plus reliable calculations along with those based on statistical analyses of existing data alone. Some 262 drawings of the mass-chain decay scheme are included. The tabular entries for each isotope are ordered by increasing atomic number. For all nuclear science research collections. (RGK)

Tables of physical and chemical constants and some mathematical functions. 15th ed. Originally compiled by G. W. C. Kay and T. H. Laby. Now prepared under the direction of an Editorial Committee. New York: Longman; 1986. 477p. $39.95. ISBN 0-582-46354-8. (Distributed by Wiley under ISBN 0-470-20662-4.)

This new edition still provides (since 1911) a heavy volume and wide range of physical and chemical data required for everyday laboratory purposes. Thus it is not only for specialists but more generally for scientists working in a variety of fields. For this edition new sections have been added. e.g., wavelength standards, cosmic rays, atomic radii, and calorific values of fuels. The mathematical function section, while appropriate, is very slim indeed (less than 2% of the total pages of data). (RGK)

Wörterbuch der Wasserchemie. Dictionary of water chemistry. Dictionnaire de la chimie de l'eau. By Friedrich von Ammon. Weinheim, FDR; Deerfield Beach, FL: VCH Verlagsgellschaft; 1985. 203p. $58.00. ISBN 0-89573-434-6 (U.S.A.)

Promoted by the Water Chemistry Section of the German Chemical Society, this German, English, French dictionary is meant to reflect international standardization of procedures and the establishment of water quality guidelines. Its audience is expected to be professionals in the field of water chemistry who need an aid for translations. Coverage includes all important terms related to water composition and quality, water purification, all areas of water chemistry, plus terms basic to hydrology, geology, physical and biological processes, and water technology. American terms have cross-references leading to the British spellings. The vinyl cover makes it easy to leave open for consultation. (BL)

SCIENCE, GENERAL

Corporate technology directory. Welleslley Hills, MA: Corporate Technology Information Services, Inc.; 1986. 3 vols. $750.00 per set. ISBN 0-936507-03-9.

This large set of data about organizations involved in high technology provides information about 12,500 or more manufacturers. The range of products they produce is great, including such diverse items as fiber optics, computer software, cable connectors, or amino plastics. For each organization there is the usual directory type information (name, address, staff size, sales range, and list of executives), but the main value is in the coding of high tech products each produces. Products are coded by a unique system developed for the set; it is an alphanumeric system with mnemonic features. For example, the coding for a particular material would be MAT-AB-A, representing the abrasive aluminum oxide. There are 3,000 such codes. The citations for companies occupy two volumes while the index volume provides access by names of key executives (over 42,500 of them), by product code (over 40,000 of those), by zip codes, by key words of products (such as abrasive materials, alumimum oxide for the example used above), and by name of parent companies where there is one. All in all it should be very useful to sci-tech libraries needing a specialized directory for reaching the high-tech organizations in the U.S. It is also available as an online database or a magnetic tape for in-house use. (EM)

Fire prevention handbook. By Derek James. Boston: Butterworths; 1986. 146p. $37.95. ISBN 0-408-02260-4.

This is a practical book about fire prevention in commerce and industry written for the small to medium-sized operation. The author lays down the rules and shows how good housekeeping, training, and motivation can contribute much to the prevention of fire. Though the work is of British origin and many examples are from the United Kingdom, it can be a worthy, albeit nontechnical, support for evaluating industrial fire safety plans and operations. (RGK)

International computer vision directory. Edited by Philip C. Flora. Conroe, TX: Technical DataBase Corp. Blue Ridge Summit, PA: TAB; 1985. 156p. $34.00. ISBN 0-910747-08-3 (pbk).

Each software listing (there are over 150) includes the necessary information for easy product comparison. Included too is a company description on each software vendor. There are two indexes: one by company name and one by software application. For comprehensive computer science collections in industry. (RGK)

Pacific research centers: a directory of organizations in science, technology, agriculture, and medicine. London: Longman: 1986. 514p. $200.00. ISBN 0-582-90028-X.

Provides directory type information for about 3,500 organizations dealing with medicine, agriculture, technology, and science in Japan, China, Australia, New Zealand, the Phillipines, and other countries. Entries include a rather detailed paragraph describing the activities of the organizations; they are arranged alphabetically by countries. There are corporate centers, university research units, government laboratories, and independent research organizations. The book has two indexes, one by names or titles of organizations and the other by subjects. (EM)

Scientific and technical organizations and agencies directory. 1st ed. supplement. Edited by Margaret Labash Young. Detroit: Gale; 1986. 1751p. $80.00 ISBN 0-8103-2101-7.

This book serves to continue the listings given in the first edition of the two-volume work bearing this title. In this supplement are descriptions of around 2,600 organizations, following the style of the previous volumes, such as name, sponsor, foundling date, languages used, and purpose. Of the 13 chapters in this supplement, the first three deal with international organizations located outside the United States. The remaining 10 chapters list organizations whose members are involved with rather specific scientific or technical fields, such as electrotechnical information, nuclear information, and water supply/sanitation matters. There is one index including both an alphabetical listing of organizational names as well as a keyword index using terms found in organizational names. Contains a wealth of information and should serve as a handy reference tool in serious sci-tech libraries. (EM)

(The) who's who of Nobel Price winners. Edited by Bernard S. Schlessinger and June H. Schlessinger. Phoenix, AZ: Oryx Press; 1986. 212p. $35.00./ ISBN 0-89774-193-5.

This Who's Who provides a complete listing of all Nobel Prize winners, from 1901(when the first awards were given) through 1985. Each of the 541 entries is composed of 15 fields of information such as: complete name, prize category and year of award, birth and death dates, nationality, education, career information, commentary, and a selected bibliography. There is an index arranged by nationality. Recommended for all libraries. (ADC)

SCI-TECH IN REVIEW

Karla Pearce, Editor
Giuliana A. Lavendel, Associate Editor

BROWSING

Baker, Sharon L. Overload, browsers and selections. *Library and Information Science Research*. 8(4): 315-329; 1986 October-December.

Anyone who works in a sci-tech library is familiar with the technique of browsing, one preferred by many researchers to the more "standard" modes of catalog or index searching. This paper reviews the literature on the subject, analyzes browsing as a technique, discusses research studies by Herbert Goldhor and others which attempt to measure its success, and suggests additional methods to increase users' exposure to materials. Although the methods suggested to increase browsing's effectiveness may seem more appropriate to a public library, science librarians may find this very useful as well. (KJP)

ELECTRONIC FILING SYSTEMS

Betts, Mitch. In with electronic filing systems, out with antique regulations. *Computerworld*. 20(29): 15; 1986 July 21.

The Federal Security and Exchange Commission (SEC) is trying to break ties with hard copy. Its experimental Electronic Data Gathering Analysis and Retrieval (EDGAR) filing project is proceeding slowly while the SEC revises old regulations concerning the filing of corporate reports. Paper-based concepts stand in the way; the IRS plans to store millions of returns on optical disks, but the Justice Department worries about fingerprints and signatures, which are available on paper returns. The issue of legal signatures has been solved by accepting passwords and Personal Identification Number (PIN) as equivalents. The cost of digitized graphics is also a problem, as is data tagging. A prototype AI program, the Financial Statement Analyzer, had a 94% success rate and is being considered for possible integration into the mainframe environment. (GL)

AN ONLINE SERIALS LIST

Boyce, Judith I.; Boyce, Bert R. A serials holdings list using UNIX Refer. *Special Libraries.* 78(1): 1-6; 1987 Winter.

Serials lists for consortia provide valuable information but their production can be tedious and time consuming. According to the authors, if you have access to a UNIX operating system, Refer can be used to produce, with minimal effort, a high quality list which is searchable online. They describe the LaGIN Serials Record, which contains serials records for 11 state agency libraries in the state of Louisiana. An appendix gives a small sample keyword search. Because this was originally designed for construct bibliographies for research papers, the program can also be used for that purpose. (KJP)

CONTROLLING INFORMATION OVERLOAD

Campbell, William J.; Roelofs, Larry J. The development of an intelligent user interface for NASA's scientific database. *Telematics and Informatics*. 3(3): 177-190; 1986.

Like other information centers, NASA libraries are experiencing an unparalleled increase in the amount of information which they need to control. In addition, they are now being called upon to retrieve a type of data – images, maps, three dimensional drawings – not generally retrievable in the past. To address this data management problem, NASA began the Intelligent Data Management Project. From this came the design for an intelligent user interface (IUI) using a knowledge base and expert systems concepts. Starting from selecting the database to translating the user's understanding of the problem to what the database understands, they developed a prototype IUI for plate tectonics: CRUstal Dynamics Database Expert System, or CRUDDES. All the steps involved in this project are described. (KJP)

TECHNICAL INFORMATION MARKET

Chalk, Rosemary. Privatizing tech info. *Technology Review*. 90(2): 8-9; Feb, March 1987.

NTIS could become a government-chartered, nonprofit corporation like COMSAT or the St. Lawrence Seaway. In April 1986, following the results of a study conducted at the request of the Office of Management and Budget, the Commerce Department announced that it was considering "privatizing" NTIS. Consternation spread among the library community and users, who feel that the current system is worth preserving. NTIS, which employs 350 people and ships 6 million documents per years, is almost totally user-supported. The Information Industry Association welcomes the privatization proposal, but this approach could increase the access cost of information produced with public monies. Recommendations from a Department of Commerce task force will to go OMB in time for the 1988 budget. (GL)

FINDING SMALL COMPANIES

Cheney, Deborah; Malecki, Sharon. Industrial directories, a close look. *RQ*. 26(2): 221-230; 1986 Winter.

Although not so dependent on this source as people who work in business libraries, sci-tech librarians are often called upon for information about small private companies that can only be found in industrial directories. The authors describe these directories, discuss their arrangement, their completeness, and even give the contents of those they examined. They concentrate mostly on regional directories and do not cover any that are devoted to a single industry. Since the majority of companies covered here will not be listed in sources such as the *Million Dollar Directory* or *Standard and Poor's*, this may be the only place to find listings of these companies in your area. (KJP)

SCIENCE AND TECHNOLOGY AND THE PUBLIC

Culliton, Barbara J. Science sections in U.S. newspapers increase dramatically in past 2 years. *Science*. 235(4787): 429; Jan 23.

According to a recent survey by nonprofit Scientists' Institute for Public Information, 47 dailies began publishing weekly science and technology sections between 1984 and 1986, bringing the total number of such contributions to 66. This is an impressive total, considering that an even larger number of newspapers have a weekly science page. Polled readers confirm their interest in scientific and technical matters, with medicine and health having priority. Some professionals believe that special sections "ghettoize" science, which should become part of regular news. In the same period, however, two prominent science magazines, *Science 86* and *Science Digest* have folded, raising questions about the general public's interest in science and technology. (GL)

SCHOLARLY JOURNALS

Horowitz, Irving Louis. Limits of standardization in scholarly journals. *Scholarly Publishing*. 18(2): 125-30; 1987 January.

Sales of academic journals are dropping for a host of reasons, including increased use of institutional, library, and interlibrary services. There are also a greater number of journals being published to meet the competition for tenure and to report research breakthroughs. Standardization is one measure considered to lower costs. This is aided by the new technologies and the fact that journals are now in the hands of relatively few publishes. The need for diversification, however, should not be forgotten. Factors like paid circulation, subscription price, frequency, special content, the role of professional organizations, differential style and design, and publication history all limit standardization. Publishers receive both economic and status rewards: by meaningful balance of standardization vs. diversification, a polarized decision is reduced to an everyday sort of problem. (GL)

"HARD" VS. "SOFT" SCIENCE

Houser, Lloyd. The classification of science literatures by their "hardness." *Library and Information Science Research*. 8(4): 357-372; 1986 October-December.

In this critical review of key studies of the criteria for hard and soft science, the author discusses attempts by librarians to classify science literatures. This subject has interested librarians because it can provide a means of organizing collections more efficiently for their users. Houser discusses the work of Janet Chase, Warren Hagstrom, William McGrath, Derek Price, Norman Storer, and Thomas Kuhn; but he finds their conclusions to be too speculative and subjective. Their approach, using a checklist of characteristics, is invalid both historically and philosophically; he suggests instead Toumoulin's evolutionary approach. (KJP)

NETWORK COLLABORATION

Karon, Paul. Worldwide computer organization capitalizes on independent networks. *PC Week*. 3(51): 37,44; 1986 December 23/30.

The oldest (40 years) and the largest (78,000 members) association of computer practitioners is dedicated to the science and art of information processing. Headquartered in New York City, The Association for Computing Machinery (ACM) issues a dozen journals and organizes 60 conferences (with proceedings) per years, including those built around Special Interest Groups or SIGs. Since key members of the organization are scattered throughout the world, ACM has replaced telephones and switchboards with electronic mail, using Local Area Networks and large utilities like ARPANET. Paper communications have been virtually eliminated within the organization. Electronic submittal of manuscripts over the network and on floppies is being practiced. Since standardization is a problem, ACM faces the possibility of getting input into a standard langauge of editorial notations. The American Association of Publishers is now working on a standard generalized markup formula with universal symbols. (GL)

A BASIC EXPERT SYSTEM

Owen, John Mackenzie. Helping the user by computer: a BASIC program. *Library Software* Review. 4(5): 224-227; 1986 July-August.

HELP is a menu-driven, knowledge-based, hierarchical program with the goal of providing beginning level library information. This information includes: library rules and hours; how to use the subject catalog; how to use reference materials, bibliographies, journals, and newspapers; and how to find recommended readings. The actual BASIC program for the "help" command is included, along with suggestions for modifying the program to a particular library's own use. This is a tool that can relieve the librarian of routine instructional and directional tasks, provide an informal communication system with the library, and help train new staff. (KJP)

ARTIFICIAL INTELLIGENCE

Stefik, Mark. The next knowledge medium. *The AI Magazine*. 7(1): 34-45; 1986 Spring.

Artificial intelligence technology, the goal of which is to build thinking machines, could change civilization dramatically by providing an interactive knowledge medium—an information network for the generation, distribution, and consumption of knowledge. This paper is divided in three sections: stories, models, and predictions. The stories relate to mankind's evolving cultures. At the end of the Pleistocene age, hunting culture spread at a rate greater than one thousand miles per century, while the more complex farming culture spread across Europe at a rate slower than 100 miles per century. In France, railroads were introduced between 1870 and 1914, and this caused the transformation of "peasants into Frenchmen." Population genetics, ecology, economics, and scientific communities are examined as models to establish parameters for the author's forecasts. Books are passive knowledge media, while expert systems based on AI both store and supply knowledge. Examples of expert systems, like Colab, the author's experiment in team computing, are cited. (GL)

For Product Safety Concerns and Information please contact our EU
representative GPSR@taylorandfrancis.com
Taylor & Francis Verlag GmbH, Kaufingerstraße 24, 80331 München, Germany

www.ingramcontent.com/pod-product-compliance
Lightning Source LLC
Chambersburg PA
CBHW052119300426
44116CB00010B/1721